Smiling Again

Smiling Again

Coming Back to Life and Faith after Brain Surgery

Sally Stap

NEW YORK

Smiling Again

Coming Back to Life and Faith After Brain Surgery

Published in New York, New York, by Morgan James Publishing. Morgan James and The Entrepreneurial Publisher are trademarks of Morgan James, LLC. www.MorganJamesPublishing.com

The Morgan James Speakers Group can bring authors to your live event. For more information or to book an event visit The Morgan James Speakers Group at www.TheMorganJamesSpeakersGroup.com.

A **free** eBook edition is available with the purchase of this print book.

CLEARLY PRINT YOUR NAME ABOVE IN UPPER CASE

Instructions to claim your free eBook edition:
1. Download the BitLit app for Android or iOS
2. Write your name in **UPPER CASE** on the line
3. Use the BitLit app to submit a photo
4. Download your eBook to any device

ISBN 978-1-61448-796-8 paperback
ISBN 978-1-61448-797-5 eBook
Library of Congress Control Number:
2013944423

Cover Photo by:
Sally Stap

Cover Design by:
Chris Treccani
www.3dogdesign.net

Interior Design by:
Bonnie Bushman
bonnie@caboodlegraphics.com

In an effort to support local communities and raise awareness and funds, Morgan James Publishing donates a percentage of all book sales for the life of each book to Habitat for Humanity Peninsula and Greater Williamsburg.

Get involved today, visit
www.MorganJamesBuilds.com

Habitat
for Humanity®
Peninsula and
Greater Williamsburg
Building Partner

To MY Family, without whom I would have given up.

"God didn't desert us——He gave us a sense of humor."

—Fred Stap

"I have seen the hand of God——may He continue to guide hands at the Mayo Clinic."

—Allen Stap

The Path

Introduction:

Waking to a Nightmare

It surprised me how quickly consciousness came after surgery. A nurse said, "You're awake," from behind me. She offered a wet sponge to my mouth. I eagerly sucked water to moisten my parched mouth. She seemed to know what I needed before I thought it. I saw a clock, and calculated eleven hours since my last memory. Eleven hours in brain surgery to remove a 2.8 cm Acoustic Neuroma (AN). How bad had the tumor been, I wondered? The room was bright, quiet with the exception of my beeping equipment. It was late and I was alone in Recovery at Mayo Clinic in Rochester, Minnesota.

Back pain was first, aching beyond description. My left hip burned. Lying on my side for so long with my head in a vice had twisted my body. I didn't expect pain so far from my head. Then discomfort invaded my head and neck so intensely that I couldn't lay still. I said "my back" but it came out "my ack." Something had happened to my mouth. The nurse apologized for making me repeat myself, finally understood, and quickly added pillows beneath me.

Why was she repeatedly putting drops in only my right eye? It sank in that the worst HAD happened. The right side of my face was paralyzed. I had read about facial paralysis, but I had disregarded it. A paralyzed face doesn't allow the eye to blink properly so keeping my eyes closed was most comfortable. I did a mental inventory, which I was aware enough to know was a good sign. Where was God? Why hadn't my prayers been answered? I'd made it out alive, but my prayer for no complications was going unanswered. This wasn't looking good for my prayer warriors. So much for the glowing testimony that I had planned.

Two residents were suddenly talking to me. They were in my face, eager to assess my condition. They asked me to smile, but only one side of my teeth showed. They asked me to raise my eyebrows, but only one lifted. They asked me to close my eyes, but the right didn't fully close. This couldn't be! I threw up instantly when one asked me to follow his finger with my eyes. I had no control of my body as it was consumed by heaving. My head was raw with pain. I slowly opened my eyes to see that the residents were gone. They must have been satisfied with my responses. They confirmed that I could follow directions, my brain was confused about balance, and my face was paralyzed on the right side. My vestibular system had been assaulted.

The nurse kept asking me if I was in pain. *YES*, I thought, but I nodded. I was starting to feel every inch of my body. The anesthesiologist had told me that I would only be given medication "to take the edge off" because they needed me to be alert enough to know if something was going wrong in my head. He was right. I was incredibly alert inside a body that resembled a coma patient splayed out with IV lines, oxygen tubes, and a heart monitor.

I wondered about my family. Eleven hours was gone in an instant for me, but how about them? Were they okay? How did they spend the hours? What had the doctors told them?

Intensive Care

I was afraid of motion as the bed rolled through the hallway and up the elevator from the Recovery Room to the ICU. I did not want to get sick again. My research prepared me to have balance destroyed by surgery. I expected dizziness. I closed my eyes. Would this pain ever subside?

Where was God? Maybe a bit in the gentleness of the nurse who showed a sense of urgency to give me pain medication? Maybe in the compassionate words of the transportation guy who showed caution with every bump.

In the ICU, an entourage of people converged on me. Four or five people scrubbed me. They talked to one another about me in the third person. I heard every word but still had my eyes closed. One said that my family had become very anxious about me, so they needed to get me cleaned quickly. Washcloths were used to clean up what must have been blood, brain debris, and fluids from my body. I wondered if the doctor's initials were still written on my head with marker to ensure they drilled the correct side of my skull. Someone remarked about how bloody I was. My rag doll body was carefully lifted and shifted. They were gentle, but I screamed involuntarily whenever they touched my left hip.

Where was God? Maybe in the empathy that the team showed as they expressed care in cleaning my battered body. Their concern that I looked good for my family. Or maybe in the seamless teamwork and professionalism of the nursing team.

Eventually, they had me changed to a fresh hospital gown and new sheets. They tucked me in with fresh-smelling blankets, and one bent close to say that they were going to let my family in. The door opened and I saw three cautious loved ones approach my bed. I felt great comfort when they entered the room. "I won't be able to make it to dinner tonight...."

Kayla, my twenty-four-year-old daughter, was concerned, gingerly approaching me to hear better, "What?"

"We discussed dinner this morning. It looks like I can't make it."

She laughed, clearly with relief. My big brother Al and Dad chuckled.

"She's still got her sense of humor." Al checked each monitor with knowledge gained during a prior EMT career.

Kayla smiled and told me about the doctors. It was good news—the tumor was fully removed. I felt the aches and pains setting in. She told me that Dad had been walking laps in the hall when concerned that hours had passed between seeing the doctors and being allowed in to see me.

After a while they spoke in whispers just out of range, and I wondered what they were saying. I didn't know that they'd agreed to wait until morning to let the doctor tell me the bad news about my face. They didn't know that I had already figured it out. The truth hung heavily in the air—disappointment with the outcome mixed with relief that I was still alive. My father looked sad and tired as he kissed my forehead and said, "It's okay, baby."

I was awake and aware, but it was easiest to keep my eyes closed and not speak. My family left. I was alone with my thoughts, although an ICU nurse was nearby, ready to take any actions necessary to keep me alive.

Where was God? Not answering my prayers for no complications, but providing comfort, care, and support. I was touched, even in my pain, by the gentleness of the nurse's manner through the night. I craved every human interaction. It made me feel connected.

Reality sank in. Knowing that I was lucky to be alive didn't help that night. Each bit of reality hit the bottom of my stomach like a rock. I sank deeper and deeper into an unbelievable new self. Where was God?

A Very Long Week

For the next week in the hospital, I didn't feel much emotion due to the narcotics. I recall sadness and gratefulness. Sadness without emotion. Gratefulness every time I was touched by a nurse, family member, or through comments on my blog. I tapped into my memory for extensive research that I had done prior to surgery. It had told me that many things could go wrong, with each person experiencing a unique outcome. I had naively clung to the cases that had gone well.

I took inventory of my new reality. I learned that the tumor had been "very sticky" and difficult to remove. It had been stuck to my brain stem and facial nerve. I knew I was lucky to be alive. Each bit of truth hit me in my defenselessness, and I was sinking deeper and deeper into an unbelievable new self. How would I adjust to life with single-sided deafness? Was I really going to have to live with this tinnitus that was roaring in my head? Would the headaches ever end? Did I understand the impact of even temporary facial paralysis? I learned that it would take at least a year or more for my face to move again—if it ever did. Really?

The right side of my mouth did nothing. I couldn't drink. I struggled to use straws, painfully obvious to nurses who waited patiently. They provided gentle coaching as I tried repeatedly to figure out how to take pills. I learned to hold the right side of my lips closed with one hand and hold the straw to the left with the other.

I didn't understand the impact or danger of having one eye that wouldn't close by itself. When the doctor suggested sewing a weight into my eyelid I realized with a sickening clarity that this paralysis was not going to be short term. Ensuring the health of a cornea with no tears would require constant drops. If not, I could lose the eye, I was told countless times. The first time I looked in the mirror I didn't recognize the woman reflected with her sagging, immobile right cheek. With eyes that didn't blink in sync with one another. With sad and resigned eyes, an immobile expression. When a nurse asked me to sign a consent form for eyelid surgery I learned that I could no longer write. My right hand didn't do what I asked it to and my attempted signature looked unintelligible. How would I survive another surgery, even a minor one?

The pain and outcome were unthinkable. Giving up sounded like a good alternative to me. "No," Kayla told me. I couldn't give up. She pointed out positive things. The good news that I was still me. I had awareness of myself and memories of my life. It was "just physical stuff"—much of which would become more natural over time. Some of which would heal. I was still alive. I wondered if her pep talks were helping her as much as me. She made me laugh about things. I was incredibly proud of my daughter. When had she grown into such an amazing young woman? I didn't want to disappoint her. I felt her fighting to have her mother back by pushing me to take one more drink, bite of food, or step in the hallway.

I talked to my mother in Michigan. She was *very* cheerful and asked if I was relieved to have the surgery over with. I answered yes, but deducted that she had no idea what I was really going through. I assumed my father had filtered what he told her. I talked to my youngest daughter Kendra, twenty-two, in France and enjoyed hearing her voice. I didn't really know what to say and wondered if she could understand me without the "b" sound that I could no longer make. She was cheerful but tentative, having heard details from her sister. I hoped she knew it was okay that she was far away and not here with me. I felt her empathy and knew it was hard for her. Our conversations were a handful of slowly enunciated words.

Every day, I felt pain and discouragement roll over me in waves that left me drowning. I couldn't escape. I couldn't catch my breath. Sleep provided short breaks. I was normal and pain free for brief moments of unconsciousness, woken abruptly by pain when I moved. I fought back. One wave at a time. One challenge at a time. I couldn't give up. My family was accepting me. They still loved me. They still needed me. I could feel it. My family was fighting back their despair and being positive. I knew that when they left the room they cried, but they always came in with a smile. It made me love them even more. I had to fight. I couldn't disappoint my family. I didn't cry, even from my despair. I had to win this one—I survived a brain tumor. This was an experience bigger than me, and begging to be told.

So I wrote this book for a lot of reasons. I wanted to capture what I was going through as I experienced it. I wanted to show others that there is hope after what seems to be a hopeless situation. I wanted to capture my feelings, both emotional and physical, so I could look back and say, "See, it does get better." I sure didn't know what God was thinking, but I had faith enough to know that at some point I would be able to look back and see things differently. I saw clear evidence that God was there in subtle ways, not just through the care of others accompanying me on this journey. Throughout the book, you'll see those lessons I learned along the way that I treasure to this day. I hope they encourage you as well.

Lesson Learned

Be optimistic, but don't discount possible outcomes just because they don't sound fun.

Chapter 1

A Diagnosis from Left Field

L et's back up a bit. I grew up in a little Michigan town with dreams of not much more than getting by in life. While bouncing around, trying to decide what to do with my life, I discovered computer programming at the community college. It was love at first sight and I dove in, never looking back. With a degree in computer science from Western Michigan University in Kalamazoo, I accepted a job at The Upjohn Company, *the* place to work at the time. I loved technology and built my own computer, from motherboard to modem card, shortly after PCs came into the world. I was a geek.

I spent many years in corporate information technology (IT) as a programmer and advanced into management. When car phones came out, I immediately had one bolted to the console of my little Subaru. It was heavily used. As mobile phones advanced, I always acquired the latest technology as soon as possible. I talked on the phone almost daily as it allowed me extra work time while getting to or from work. I traveled a lot during my career and again depended on mobile technology in an attempt to "do it all."

Technology allowed me to squeeze more time out of each day. It was always my goal to be home for dinner and evening activities as my two daughters grew up. It was in the Kalamazoo area that I married, raised kids, divorced, and focused on my career. In late 2003, my job was phased out in a corporate merger. I went home and didn't know what to do. I couldn't do *nothing*—I didn't know how.

After a few restless months off, I moved to Princeton, New Jersey, for a job that eventually led to me joining a consulting firm, The W Group, based in Philadelphia. It was a wonderful opportunity, and I loved what I did. I traveled extensively to assist corporations in optimizing IT spending decisions. I spent most Mondays in airports heading somewhere and Thursday evenings returning home. If local, I spent hours in the car driving to clients in the Philadelphia area.

For a few years, I had been experiencing ringing in my ears. While driving from Princeton to Philadelphia daily, I began to notice I could hear my cell phone better if held to my left ear. Following an eighteen-month assignment for a Philadelphia area client, I commuted to southern California weekly for seven months for my next assignment. I invested in Bose noise-cancelling headphones to protect my ears from frequent air travel noise. I noticed when I got home at the end of each week after taking the redeye flight, listening to Jim Brickman and Jimmy Buffett on my Blackberry, my ears would be ringing louder for the weekend.

I meant to ask my doctor about it at my annual physical, but would forget. I assumed I would be told it was just due to my age and frequent travel. I tried a few over-the-counter remedies to no avail. Each year, I would make a mental note to ask again the following year.

In November 2007, I moved back to Michigan, to be closer to family. I started commuting weekly to Philadelphia for a long-term project assisting with vendor management. It was a busy but good routine, and I loved the work I was doing. I leased an apartment in the Philadelphia area to eliminate the need to carry luggage weekly. It was a great little apartment, and I settled in quickly. I loved my life. I was doing what I had dreamed of—consulting, traveling, adding value.

In early 2008, my right eye started watering. Sometimes both eyes watered. I started to have a strange sensation on my face. Even when my right eye wasn't watering, it felt like it was. I started to feel like the right corner of my mouth was drooling. It wasn't, but the sensation was always there. I blamed herbal facial products I was using, so I started switching products. It would improve for a while and then return. It had to be something I was doing in my routine!

I failed to gain any improvement in my hearing despite over-the-counter products, headphones, and even ear candling. I definitely had less hearing in the right ear. It wasn't just ringing, and it wasn't just road noise. I did research on the Internet and didn't find much, but I learned that sometimes the three little bones in the ear are messed up. I also heard sometimes calcium builds up in the ear. So I decided to get a hearing test to determine if there really was a difference and to have a baseline for later in life when I might need a hearing aid.

I went to a hearing center at the end of July to have my hearing tested. The audiologist asked me if I had any numbness on my face. I immediately said no because I hadn't connected my facial sensations to numbness. I sat in a grey soundproof booth, with wires coming from each ear. I saw the audiologist and clearly heard his prompts in each ear. I noticed I heard more sounds in my left ear than my right one. Afterward, as I looked at the audiology report showing a definite difference between the lines representing my two ears, the audiologist explained that travel and age should affect both ears equally. I had a marked difference in the right ear. He recommended I see an ear-nose-throat specialist (ENT) because it could be something treatable, or even something as serious as a brain tumor.

While I was confident I didn't have a brain tumor, I did take his advice to have it further checked out. In the car going home, it struck me that the weird sensations on my face could be described as numbness—a numbness I had dismissed as insignificant. A strange feeling in my gut started to develop.

Clues from the Past

I didn't allow myself to think it could be a brain tumor. In the past, I had let my imagination get the better of me when waiting for test results and didn't want to do that again. Slowly, over time, I started to remember things, seemingly insignificant at the time, from the past. In 2001, I had strange little bursts of pinging sounds in my brain and wondered. Around the same time, I went to the doctor with severe vertigo and was told I was suffering effects of flying. For several days, I had to touch a wall to steady myself, and slept with a foot on the floor to stop the room from spinning. I fought it, it went away, and I regained my balance. I realized my eyes had looked different in pictures for the past few years. The right eye had, over time, started to be opened wider. I started to connect the dots.

Following my hearing test, I made an appointment with an ENT, but it wasn't until September that I could get in due to my work schedule. Having to make all appointments on Fridays when I was home was difficult. I pushed everything to the back of my mind. The urgency was starting to build for me to find out what was going on. The gut feeling that something was seriously wrong was growing.

Finally, September came. I was working from home for the Labor Day week, so I had an appointment with the ENT on Tuesday. The doctor was an energetic lady who I instantly liked. She asked me if I was ever dizzy, and I said no. Not since 2001. She handed me a brochure and said it might be Meniere's disease. There is no cure, but things like cutting salt can minimize the symptoms. Gee, how encouraging. She turned to my patient records, and I saw her write three simple letters: "MRI." She wanted to eliminate anything "scary" before we proceeded with a diagnosis. My appointment lasted about ten minutes.

She sent me off with a brochure on Meniere's disease, the MRI phone number, and a mid-October appointment to review the findings. I had plans to go to Mackinac Island with my family that weekend. On Monday, I had a flight back to Philadelphia for work. So I sandwiched an MRI into Sunday evening at 7:00 PM. I was too busy to have anything seriously wrong with me.

Nine of us headed north to Mackinac Island. It is between the lower and upper sections of Michigan. We wandered around the picturesque little town on the island that allows only horses and bikes—no motorized vehicles. I remember sitting on the porch of an old building in Fort Mackinac watching rain fall steadily during one of many showers that day. My brother joined me as the others went into the gift shop or were trapped in other buildings by the sudden downpour. "I have an MRI tomorrow night. There's a chance I have a brain tumor."

He asked a few questions, but then said, "Don't worry, it will probably be nothing."

We sat quietly, watching the rain, each processing our own thoughts.

Sunday morning came, and nine of us headed south. Back to life, and back to reality.

The Test and Long-Awaited Results

The MRI had a little mirror in it, which kept me from being too claustrophobic in the large, white, tubular machine. I didn't know what to expect. I heard a series of loud banging noises. The operator told me how long each series would be through a speaker in the tube. There were several people in the control room chatting while one guy kept an eye on his computer monitor. Then the room was empty except for the one intently watching his screen. Did that mean anything? No, it probably meant a shift change. Half way through, a man came in to inject contrast dye into my arm. He asked me if I was doing okay. I assume they ask everyone that, but I felt like he was handling me with kid gloves. After about forty-five minutes it was over. I was dismissed and heading home to pack for two weeks of work. I pushed the concerns away, and dove into life. I would find out in October what they had found. Nothing, I assumed. I told myself if the doctor was *really* concerned, she would have given me an appointment sooner.

Kendra came with me to Philadelphia the next day. She had graduated from University of Michigan that spring and was hanging out with me until she left for eight months in France. She speaks fluent French and was going to teach English as a second language in an elementary school. I was excited to have her come with me to Philadelphia for a week. Through the years I had frequently taken my daughters with me on work travels, so she knew the routine and would fit right in with a mixture of alone time and Mom time. She could meet my colleagues and see my Philadelphia apartment. We had a company meeting in downtown Philadelphia scheduled Thursday and Friday, which would give her an opportunity to explore the city. She would stay the weekend, and head home Sunday. I would stay through the second week for work, and head home Thursday evening.

Two days after the MRI, on Tuesday, September 9, 2008, at about 11:15 AM, I got a call from the doctor's office. I will always remember the specific date, time, and how it felt to get a life-changing call. I was sitting at my desk. The doctor's appointment secretary told me they had found "something abnormal" on my MRI, and I needed to come right in to see the doctor. I told her I was out of town for two weeks, so I wasn't sure how quickly I could get in. She said it was urgent and the doctor would make time any day for me. Wow. A "kick in the gut" moment. I remember the piece of paper I was scribbling on. Taking notes, "Any day, anytime", "something abnormal." Brain tumor came to mind, but it was unthinkable. I told myself it was something less severe. She probably found something wrong with the bones in my ear.

I told her I had plans that week, but would come home Sunday and meet with the doctor on Monday. I was protecting the time I had with my daughter and afraid that once I saw the doctor my busy bubble would burst. I thought of jumping on a plane right away, but it seemed to be overreacting. Making a big deal with the client about leaving work early would end up embarrassing. It was better to keep quiet.

After hanging up the phone, I sat for a minute trying to catch my breath. I didn't want to cry in my office. *Any day, any time. Something abnormal.* I took deep breaths. I left my desk, and just started walking down the hall between rows of cubicles. I remember turning left. Not going anywhere, but needing to not be where I was. Maybe the bathroom. Maybe outdoors. Amy, a client colleague, paused to ask me a question, and then stopped and stared at me. "Are you okay?"

"Well, no. I just heard from my doctor and I don't know what's up. They said it's urgent that I return for something 'abnormal' on my MRI. Please don't say anything." I didn't intend to talk about it to anyone, but she came along at just the right time.

"Absolutely. I survived breast cancer and can still remember getting the diagnosis." She told me about hearing her diagnosis and then about the positive outcome after treatment. She was a great comfort. She offered that if I needed anything to let her know.

"Thank you, Amy. I'll let you know. Hopefully I'll be right back here next week and it will have been nothing."

Just telling someone helped. I could breathe again. I know God sent her down the hall at work that day to ensure she would run into me. I can't say how much it calmed me. I knew cancer was an option, but couldn't believe anything serious with such minor symptoms. I felt fine!

I worked the rest of that day and Wednesday. Every meeting found me preoccupied with the upcoming doctor visit. What could it be that they found abnormal? I watched time tick by on clocks. I watched mouths move. Life was normal for everyone but me. Trees outside the conference rooms were green. Would I see them the following week?

I did an Internet search on brain tumors but the topic was too broad and overwhelmed me. I sent a note to my parents telling them I was coming home on Sunday with Kendra for a doctor's appointment. I told Kayla I had something abnormal on my MRI. I told Kendra too, but we pushed it out of our minds. As much as we could.

Having Kendra with me that week was a great comfort. We didn't talk much about the possible outcomes, but having her there calmed me. I think God planned that also. While I wanted to freak out and cry, having my daughter with me kept me together. I kept reminding myself that I was her mother, and I couldn't allow her to be scared. She needed to see me strong. Later, Kayla and Kendra told me they had talked during the week. They knew it had to be serious, but they weren't prepared for a brain tumor.

Company meetings on Thursday and Friday were a great time to see everyone I work with, as we were normally spread out over the continent at various consulting jobs. We laughed a lot during the evenings at dinner. I told a couple of friends that I might have a brain tumor. Their reaction that I might be overreacting calmed me. All the time, I was incredibly happy and kept taking mental snapshots to remember the fun we had. Laughing over a glass of wine. Chuckling about a wisecrack. My work colleagues loved Kendra, and she was made to feel like part of the family.

Saturday was spent shopping with Kendra. We bought posters for my apartment. We bought a ridiculous tree lamp, about 5 feet tall and a challenge to take home. I thought about the abnormal test. If it was bad, I would be closing up the apartment. So something told me not to decorate, but I couldn't stop. Continuing normally kept me together. I had a headache, and realized I had been experiencing more headaches recently. I was paranoid. One minute I had a brain tumor causing headaches. The following moment was fine with the doctor overreacting about something minor. I would tell myself I was crazy and headaches were from the stress of waiting.

Finally Sunday came and we flew home to Michigan. Due to thunderstorms rolling through the Midwest, our plane was diverted and then delayed. I tossed and turned for most of the night.

Monday morning was slow. I spent time in my home office doing work. Keeping my life normal and on track. I wondered out loud what the doctor could possibly want to talk about. Kendra looked normal externally, but was clearly concerned. Neither of us dared to say out loud what it might be.

I kept looking at the clock. It occurred to me that I should have someone come with me to the doctor's appointment, but didn't want to show alarm. It was important to keep it together. It was important to handle it alone. Little did I know how wrong I was and how blessed I would be soon by the people in my life.

Kendra had an eye doctor's appointment at the same time as my appointment. I thought having my parents come with me was definitely overkill. Asking Kayla to drive an hour to go with me would have been absolutely ridiculous. Finally, the time came, and I said good luck to Kendra. We headed our separate ways to two very different appointments.

I arrived at the hospital reassuring myself it was going to be nothing. It wasn't going to be a brain tumor. What if I had cancer? Would I go through treatment? In my mind, a brain tumor was a death sentence. I was going to be brave and refuse to go through difficult treatments. The next minute I was dismissing that as a diagnosis. I looked calm sitting in the waiting room but inside I was panicking. *This is a big deal. No, it will be nothing. This is a big deal.* The doctor's mother was an artist, and the walls of the waiting room were lined with large and colorful art. Strangely out of place, wonderfully distracting flowers and landscapes.

A nurse called my name.

I rose quickly and followed her through a door into the office.

"Thanks for coming in."

"No problem, I mean, I think. I guess we'll find out."

We both laughed nervously. She led me to an examining room, clearly uncomfortable and aware of whatever "it" was.

As I waited for the doctor in the examining room, I could hear her voice out in the hallway saying something about the big screen … public … she was going to go "tell her."

She confidently swept into the room. She was warm but nervous. She got right to it. After greeting me, before even sitting down, she told me I had a benign brain tumor and something about acoustic something. I immediately stopped her and asked how they knew it was benign. I was so incredibly relieved by that one word that it softened the brain tumor part. She said it was a well-known tumor, so they knew with a high degree of certainty it was benign. She said something about losing my hearing, and then discounted it. "People can get by quite well with one ear."

What? She then said they were going to refer me to Mayo Clinic in Rochester, Minnesota. The type of brain tumor I had, an acoustic neuroma, required a specialty team I could only find in certain hospitals. Nobody in Kalamazoo would want to do it. It occurred in only one in 100,000 people worldwide, or about 3,000 cases a year in the United States.

What? My head was spinning. It was good because it was benign. It was bad because it was a brain tumor. It was good because if you get a brain tumor, this is the kind to get because I would only lose hearing in one ear. Why was that good? I guess because I would live? I stared at a tattered magazine lying on a table, clearly outdated with bright orange and red flowers on the cover.

She offered to show me the MRI image on her laptop privately, or on a bigger screen in the hallway. I was numb. I wasn't worried about crying. I was fine with the bigger screen in the hallway. I prepared myself to be confused by the MRI image assuming I would have trouble making out where the tumor was on the screen in abstract blobs of stuff.

She led me out to the hallway and showed me a large computer screen displaying an image of a brain, my brain. I almost lost my closely held guard and inhaled sharply when I saw an obvious and large white blob in the middle of the image. Surrounded by abstract blobs of stuff. I laughed and said, "Well, I guess I don't have to ask you where the tumor is." There was a large, white, balloon imbedded between my brainstem and right ear. Since it was situated between the two ears evident on the image, I said, "Well, I guess we now know why the wind doesn't blow through from ear to ear."

We stared. I didn't know what to ask. After a week of nonstop questions I was question less. My eyes drifted to the corner of the image to see my name, clearly showing this was all true. I diverted my thoughts and comments to the program being used to project the image, tapping into my computer science background. "Wow that's pretty cool software." I was maintaining my external cool, but felt myself starting to fall apart inside. "Can I get a copy of this image?"

She had a copy of the written lab report for me, but directed me to get a CD of the images from the records department at the hospital.

I was aware of nurses in the background trying to be invisible. I could see them out of my peripheral vision, quiet as they slipped past. It was clear everyone in the office knew what the doctor was telling me. They had been waiting a week just like me. It was abnormally quiet. The numbness was starting to wear off. I was going to cry.

We returned to the examining room. I sat down, and started to formulate questions. I had trouble controlling my voice, not trusting it but needing to get information. I sobbed. The doctor gave me a Kleenex, clearly uncomfortable. She asked if I had any questions. I asked questions. She couldn't answer them. This unusual brain tumor was clearly out of her area of specialty. I asked about hospitalization time, recovery time, outcomes. Her information was outdated, so I really needed to ask the doctors at Mayo.

She said they had not contacted Mayo yet because they thought it was important to tell me first, in person, so I didn't get any random calls from Mayo about my "brain tumor." I could tell there was nothing more she could tell me. She had referred me back to my general physician who would handle the Mayo referral. It was clear we were finished.

I didn't want to leave the room, yet I couldn't wait to be in my car. The problem was the space between. I was struggling to hold it together. There was nothing more to discuss; no reason to stay. She offered to let me sit for a while. I declined and thanked her politely. We walked into the hall. My stomach was pushing my heart out of my chest. I tried to inhale and exhale to calm myself, but my lungs caught on each inhale. I heard her behind me, taking action, "She knows. Call her physician's office and tell them to call Mayo." Her voice faded as I hurried down the hall toward the exit. The girl at the front desk told me it was no charge. I chuckled to myself, thinking they must have a special for people with brain tumors. I didn't trust my voice to share my morbid humor. I tried to smile but my lips quivered.

I quickly walked out and headed to the stairwell. I couldn't get there fast enough. As soon as I got through the door, tears came. I went quickly down the stairs toward the parking ramp. I held my breath with difficulty when passing someone coming up and I went down. I noted green walls and grey steps. Cement steps. Green railings. I had to get in my car where nobody would see me crying. I was gasping for breath while trying to calm my breathing. I held a tissue up to my eyes and nose to hold back my racing thoughts and emotions. I had a brain tumor. I hung onto the benign part. I might live through this. The doctor was quite confident I would be okay.

I got in my car and just sat for a few minutes, staring at the grey, nondescript concrete of the hospital parking ramp. I wailed. I rocked back and forth. I rested my arms and head on the steering wheel.

When the sobbing stopped, I backed out and headed home. I knew I didn't want to get on a plane for work the next day, but I didn't know what to do. I thought I was over the emotions and ready for the action plan as I drove out. I had cried for five minutes and that was enough. It was time for project mode. Get this thing out and get back to life.

I was used to handling things alone. My plan was to deal with this and move on. God's plan was different. He was already starting to show me people in my life who cared. People who would step in to help me get through this.

Chapter 2

Delivering Big News

From the car, I called one of my colleagues, Jeff. He was one of the few people who I had told I might have a brain tumor, so he was prepared. He would be a good start. I'd ask his advice on how to handle work. The thought of talking to my family was unthinkable. I thought if I practiced on someone else, I would figure out how to handle it when I got home. When Jeff answered, I lost the strength and composure I thought I had, "Do I need to go to work tomorrow if I have a brain tumor?" I was embarrassed as sobs escaped despite my attempts to control my voice and emotions. I told him about the doctor's report, and he jumped right to action, after I reassured him it really was true.

"What can I do? Do you want me to call Harry?"

"Could you? I have some family to tell right now. I booked a flight for the morning back to Philly, but I just don't think I can go to work tomorrow. But we need to let them know I won't be there and figure out what to do to cover for my absence."

"That's understandable. You shouldn't even try. I'll handle things at work. Harry and I will figure out what to do for the client."

Always the professional, I just found out I had a brain tumor, but one of my first concerns was for my client. "Good. I don't want them left hanging. But I just can't focus right now."

"Should you be driving?"

"I don't have a choice. I have to get home."

Kalamazoo had just experienced flooding near the hospital. I struggled to keep it together emotionally while turning my car around again and again because of flooded roads and clogged traffic. I tried to take the normal route but it was flooded. I had no patience for the traffic delay. I turned down a random side street and again found water. I didn't think I would ever get home. I was as overwhelmed as the flooded streets. Water blocked my drive home. A tumor blocked my future. Eventually, I wound around the city and got past the flooding. Would I eventually navigate this tumor?

I repeatedly replayed things in my head, trying to pull anything new out of the conversation I had just had with the doctor. I dreaded telling anyone. I puzzled about what all of this meant. I drove home in a daze. The doctor had made a brain tumor sound minor. She gave the impression it would be quick surgery to remove it. That didn't reconcile with my preconceived notions about brain tumors meaning death. I cried off and on all the way home. Since they knew it was benign, I wouldn't have to be brave and refuse treatment for something malignant. Because it was benign I also didn't seem to have biopsies in my future. However, I did have brain surgery coming and it was huge. They would have to get inside my skull. That didn't sound easy or painless.

As I approached my house, I sniffed and practiced a positive, smiling face. I had no idea how I was going to tell Kendra. I wondered if she was even home, as she had planned to head to Ann Arbor that afternoon to visit friends for a couple days.

I drove in the garage like any other day and parked next to Kendra's car that was still there. I inhaled and exhaled, straightened my posture, and went in the house. My two little Italian Greyhounds were at the door, as usual, eager to greet me. I spoke to them with strained excitement. "Hi Gina, hi Paulo, how are my babies?" I thought I was doing well. I went to the kitchen and heard Kendra come down the steps. As she approached, I inhaled and strategically had my back to her. "How did the appointment go?"

Hearing her weakened me. Turning and seeing her broke me. This was real. This was hard. I cried and she hugged me. I couldn't speak for a minute. I didn't trust my voice to sound confident. Instinctively, she already knew. "I'm sorry, Mom."

What could I say? I was finally was able to utter, "The good news is that my brain tumor is benign." We hugged. We cried. "I don't want to get mascara on your white shirt, Kendra. How did you know it was bad?"

"I knew something was wrong when you greeted the dogs." My voice had betrayed me. Evidently it was obvious I had been crying all the way home—go figure. I thought I had it together. She had stayed home to support me with whatever news I would come home with. I was happy she was there. I felt her strength and love.

I sat down at my desk. I'm always task oriented, and embraced having things to do. I was composed as I called my primary doctor to find out about my referral to Mayo Clinic. The operator who answered at the doctor's office said he was out. I said rather matter-of-factly, "I have a brain tumor and was told to call for a referral to Mayo."

"Yes, we have been expecting your call."

I chuckled. I guessed a brain tumor was exciting, and I visualized everyone being lined up for the past week. Waiting for me to return home so they could pull the trigger on the referral. She said she would call Mayo immediately and call me back. I told Kendra, "It must have been a slow day at the doctor's office. Having a lady with a brain tumor is big news."

I checked my e-mail. I was in task mode. That way I didn't have to feel. I had an e-mail from my mother asking me about my appointment. My family was waiting to hear. I jokingly asked Kendra if I could just send my mother an e-mail because I was dreading the conversation. I replied to the e-mail that I would be over to talk in a while. There was some good news and some bad news. I was glued to my desk waiting to hear from the doctor.

The phone rang, and it was Kayla. She was upset I hadn't called her yet. My family was circling. Kayla and Kendra had talked earlier and agreed it was probably going to be bad news. I told her I had a brain tumor, but it was benign. I repeated what the doctor said about it being one of the best types of brain tumors you can get! Talking to Kayla and Kendra was hard. Yet it was easy and it was comfort. I joked because that is what we do, but my heart was heavy in my chest. I had the MRI report from the doctor, and I read it to Kayla. While on the phone, we did Internet searches to find out what an acoustic neuroma is. It is a tumor that grows on the auditory nerve. It grows between the ear and the brainstem, pushing on the brain's cerebellum. Kayla said she would continue to research after we hung up. Kendra and I looked at each other. "I wish the nurse would return my call."

Lesson Learned

Do research to understand the possible outcomes.

My wish was granted as the phone rang again. The nurse told me I would hear from Mayo within a few days. A few days? Wasn't this everyone's top priority? Obviously not, as Mayo didn't find it as earth shaking as the local doctors.

Kendra and I wanted to understand the size of the tumor, which was measured in the MRI as 2.8 centimeters. We got out the ruler and made a life-sized model of the tumor with tangled green paper clips and bright orange earplugs. It was big! We had read the growth rate is 1 to 2 mm a year, so it had been growing inside my head for ten to fifteen years—or more.

It's Hard to Say the Words

Finally, I had nothing left to use as an excuse to not tell my parents. With dread, Kendra and I drove two miles to their house. We sat in the living room and started to chat about safe, everyday things. I didn't know how to begin. My mother did. "So, what did you find out at the doctor's appointment?"

I didn't know how to answer her. I didn't trust my voice or words. I said simply, yet fully, "I've been referred to Mayo." What a crazy thing to say. I couldn't say the words. I could feel Kendra watching me, studying how I was going to handle it.

Mom got a sick look on her face and said, "Oh, that's serious."

I said, "Well, the good news is that my brain tumor is benign."

Mom quickly rose from her chair and crossed the room to hug me as I also rose to meet her. I bent to hug my little mother who, at 5'1", was several inches shorter than me. We cried together.

Kendra didn't know what to do with herself. She looked at Dad, whose eyes were tearing up, and he said, "You're all going to make me start crying."

We regained our composure and sat again. The news was out. I told them what I knew at that point. Until I got an appointment date from Mayo Clinic, I was on hold.

My parents said my e-mail told them there was good and bad news. They had speculated good meant it was treatable. Bad meant it was probably a brain tumor. They were right on. That is what my family does. We take the good news part of everything. On that day, the action was to figure out how to get rid of this tumor. We speculated about what was going to happen.

Kendra and I eventually went home. She decided to stay overnight to be with me. We had a somewhat normal evening interjected with speculation about what was happening to me. We were in shock. I did some research on the Internet and received some e-mail research from Kayla. She and her husband lived about an hour south of me, so instead of coming over, she spent the evening researching the topic.

I called Al. "I understand that Mom called already."

"Yeah. Where did this thing come from?"

"No idea. I don't know much of anything yet. I'll let you know when I hear from Mayo."

We've always been close, but there aren't always a lot of words exchanged when we talk. Well, maybe I pass more than he returns. However, even without much spoken, I could feel the heaviness my news brought to him. I knew he would be there for anything I needed. Anything, that is, he could provide.

Kendra and I went to the grocery store. It was strange to do something normal and mundane. I wondered that other people were the same when I was going through such a dramatic life event. It felt surreal. Were the lights brighter than usual? Nobody in the store knew about my brain tumor. I put Italian bread in the cart, my favorite. I grabbed a package of cream horn pastries. As I put them in the cart, Kendra told me to stop. "You can't only buy comfort foods."

"Yes I can." We laughed that I would automatically look to comfort foods and sugar to help me through the event. I still bought the comfort food, but it exposed the weakness inside me.

I was exhausted that night, drained by the news. I was talked out, and went to bed. At 3 AM, I woke up, suddenly wide awake. The house was quiet, my two dogs and cat sleeping on the bed. I heard their breathing as they slept through my crisis. It started to sink in that I had a brain tumor, and it was unbelievable. I had nothing in the darkness to distract me. I started to cry. I decided to just let it out. Let myself feel. My body was wracked with sobs. I cried out, wailing with fear and grief. The animals slept.

Lesson Learned

Allow yourself to grieve because there is a new you. It may be pretty darn close to the old one, or possibly quite different.

I heard footsteps in the hallway. Kendra came in and crawled into bed with me. I was embarrassed, and joked, "Good luck getting past the pets." That broke the discomfort and awkwardness. "I'm glad I don't have to go to work tomorrow."

"Me too, Mom. I love you."

Eventually we drifted back to sleep. The animals slept. Sleep allowed an escape for me from the uncertainty of tomorrow.

Chapter 3

Waiting for Answers

Morning came, and I waited for the call from Mayo. I continued to do research on the Internet. I encouraged Kendra to head to Ann Arbor. I didn't want to have her put her life on hold just because mine was. Kayla offered to come over for the evening. I wondered why they thought someone needed to be with me, but I needed to be alone. It was just the beginning of the incredible support I would have from my daughters over the coming months. God reminding me I didn't have to walk alone.

As days passed, I was at a loss about how to spend time. My busyness had slowed to a crawl. I drove to the hospital and got a CD with the MRI images. I studied them on my computer. *That thing was huge!* There was nothing I could do. I jumped into action to ensure my legal paper work was in order. I contacted my attorney to update my will, my living will, and my trust. I couldn't plan my funeral. That was going too far. I didn't accept I might die.

I was most worried about the effect on my family. The girls were strong with me, and we found things to laugh about through the process (example, I named it Parry, my parasitic friend). My brother was quiet, and didn't want to look at the MRI image. My parents looked tired, and Dad was upset that it was me and not him.

I spent a day at the county fair with my parents. It was surreal to see such normalcy in the midst of my personal crisis. The horses still raced. The vendors still served food. The world did not stop because I had a brain tumor. I went to dinner and a play with one of my friends. I couldn't stop talking about "the Tumor." It loomed over anything I did to try to distract myself.

I kept thinking, "Where was God? How could life just keep going on for the rest of the world?" It's only by looking back that I would be able to see where He had been at certain points in this journey. At that point though, He was putting my mind in a numb state. A one-step-at-a-time state. I wasn't able to really deal with what was happening, so He was just holding me in His arms while we waited. I prayed. I didn't pray. I asked for strength. I asked for answers.

At the end of the week I finally got a call from Mayo Clinic. My appointment with the brain surgeons was two weeks away! I was starting to learn that hospital time is different from what I was used to in the business world. I learned that "hospital time" has its own pace.

I felt guilty about taking time off from work, but I knew I would not be able to focus on anything. My boss told me to work on getting better as fast as I could. I managed to wrap up some work for my client. I finished spreadsheets, prepared expense reports, documented things I had done, and summarized the status of things in order to ease the transition to my replacement. I assumed, of course, that it was a temporary leave. Later I would find out otherwise.

Some weeks earlier, I had signed up for a dog obedience class with my nephew and our dogs. It was a good distraction, and fun. My dog Paulo was well behaved and perfect in class. Then he promptly forgot everything he had learned when we got home each week.

I terminated my apartment lease in the Philadelphia area. My landlord waived the penalties for early termination when I explained why I wouldn't be returning. It was strange to explain to people that I had a brain tumor. It didn't feel real. I got used to saying it without emotion and became surprised at the shock it caused. Obviously, I was in a detached state. My friend Suzette packed up the apartment contents and shipped them to me in Michigan. I was conflicted, feeling I should be able to go pack it up myself, unnerved by the known existence of a brain tumor. They volunteered and I accepted.

The website for the Acoustic Neuroma Association was incredibly informative. I learned there are three options for treatment of what is commonly referred to as an "AN." The first, watch and wait, where people just watch over a certain period of time for tumor growth. Regular MRIs are used to track any growth of the tumor. If the patient has no symptoms, watching is all that is necessary.

Radiation is a second choice, with gamma knife technology. Radiation is targeted at the tumor, and causes death and eventual necrosis of the tissue. However, the tumor swells before it shrinks. Yikes.

The third option is surgical removal. The doctor had said I would need surgery, but I wondered if radiation was an option. It also appeared that if you still had hearing it could be retained. That would be dependent upon which of three entry points into the brain was used. The main area of focus for me, at that point, was losing hearing in one ear. It seemed there was high success with retaining hearing if you still had it and they entered your skull a certain way.

I spent a lot of time with my parents. We frequently went to lunch together. They were a great sounding board for me. I told them whatever

I found on the Internet. My Dad told me he had a conversation with God, asking why it couldn't have been him instead of me. We discussed surgery and radiation. We discussed possible side effects.

Where was God? I didn't really wonder at that point. In fact, I had stopped praying much. What would I ask?

I called friends who I wanted to tell personally. They were stunned to hear the news. I would generally start with chit chat and then tell them I had something I needed to tell them. I always had to work up to it. It never got easy. Eventually the words would come: "I have a benign brain tumor." Then there would be silence. They wondered what kind of sick joke I was playing on them. Then the reaction came, when they shared their disbelief. I found myself comforting them. For the brave, I e-mailed an MRI image. That usually got a reaction. For some reason, maybe my dark humor, I was amused by the reactions I got. After calling Margie, she immediately drove to my house with a super-size marble that we determined to be about the same size as the tumor.

I spent time sending e-mail to colleagues. I told them the good news was that the tumor was benign. The bad news was that I had a rather large brain tumor. Treatment options are surgery (bad haircut,) or radiation (helmet on head, zapped for hours). I told them I may lose all hearing in the right ear, and could have few or many lasting effects on some nerves (face, neck). Even while typing about the short- and long-term problems I could have, I never believed any of it would happen to me. I was confident it would sound scary but experienced minimally.

I got many encouraging notes. A lot of shocked notes. I used gallows humor to deal with a huge problem. I joked with some of them that if we got together for dinner I should pay as it could be for the last time. One of my favorite e-mails was from my friend Margie. You never know what might hit you in the salad dressing aisle.

Thanks for the update Sally! I saw Erf at Meijer's yesterday …. I didn't know if he knew about your health issue so I didn't say anything, but then I choked up in the salad dressing aisle. Since, I've talked to Nancy P. We think we should do pizza or subs or something next week … , and no, not as the "last supper," but as a shoring up for the medical times ahead. We can bring over to your house, or meet at a park.

I kept busy helping Kendra get ready to go to France for eight months. I didn't want her to go, but I also couldn't ask her to stay. It was a wonderful opportunity for her, and I had no idea what my surgery schedule would be. So off she went with the promise of talking on the phone a lot. My parents and I drove her over to the Detroit airport. I thought I would cry, but I didn't. I think I was numb.

As I watched her walk through the security line, off to a foreign country, I flashed back to seventeen years before. I remembered the details of her first day of kindergarten. She had worried about her shoelaces, so we had a little lesson that morning and she finally understood how to tie her laces. She was so proud to start school, all dressed up in her pink Minnie Mouse dress, with her hair pulled back in a ponytail and pink barrettes on the sides of her blond head. We stood and waited for what seemed like hours to her for the number 6 bus. Finally it pulled and stopped—just for her. Up the steps she went to the big scary world of school. Now, I was seeing her off at twenty-two into a bigger and scarier world, much further away.

There comes a point—years ago, and again on this day—when one has to turn and walk away. There's nothing else to see. I took a mental snapshot. After driving the two hours home, I tracked her flight online, including a status check at 1:30 AM when I awoke with my new racing thoughts.

I cleaned my house. I had lunch with friends. I rode my bike and wondered if it would be the last time. I did research on the Internet. I found videos on the Internet showing both the surgical and radiation options for treatment. Somehow I passed the time until my appointment at Mayo Clinic.

At last, the time came to go. Another sleepless night, frantic packing, and a kiss goodbye to my family and pets. Answers were getting closer. I prayed for peace, clarity, and wisdom.

Chapter 4

Taking in Mayo Clinic

Kayla accompanied me to the Mayo Clinic for my consultation appointment in early October. She was not working at the time, focusing on her MBA, so she was able to be with me throughout the process. The paperwork I received from Mayo, and clung to like a last piece of chocolate, indicated I should plan on up to a full week for testing. My initial appointment was on a Friday. So we planned for full week, including a weekend. In our nervousness, we overpacked. We had knitting, reading, laptops, and plenty of food. We assumed we would have a lot of time to kill.

We drove from Kalamazoo to Rochester, Minnesota, on Thursday evening. It took about nine hours. We were distracted and nervous. We laughed at ourselves and our nonstop speculation. We'd try to talk about different subjects, but would always find the conversation rounding back to the tumor. We speculated whether they would recommend

Lesson Learned

A sense of humor will give you a better temperament than frustration.

surgery or radiation. My research told me my tumor was considered "big," so we wondered. And we wondered some more.

The road trip was long. When I wasn't driving I watched the autumn colors along the route. I watched the white lines in the middle of the road zip past the car. I looked for normalcy in the side posts along the way. I observed the roads changing from major thoroughfares to rural Minnesota highways.

We finally arrived in Rochester. We laughed at a water tower shaped like an ear of corn. We followed the GPS as it brought us into the city that rose from flat farmland. In awe as we looked up at tall, shiny Mayo Clinic buildings. We had trouble focusing on the task of finding our hotel. After settling into our room and getting some dinner nearby, we crashed for the night. Answers were only one night's sleep away.

On Friday, October 3, it was appointment day. They didn't start until noon, so we worked out in the fitness room of the hotel. We ate breakfast. We walked around Mayo Clinic. We took pictures. Kayla took a picture of me posing with a statue of the Mayo Brothers. I had a broad, beautiful smile. It was a strange place to be sightseeing. We had an early lunch. It was only 11:30. We sat in the lobby and watched the clock. Finally it was time to check in.

When we finally were sitting in the examining room to see the doctors, we both sighed with relief. We were relieved and felt quite accomplished to have finally reached this point without going crazy. However, the wait was not over. Several minutes that felt like hours passed. Kayla took a picture of me in the examining chair. Every minute was agony. The last two weeks had been incredibly difficult, and we were about to get answers. We were in the department of otorhinolaryngology. We practiced trying to say the long name for what is ear-nose-throat medicine, or ENT. A detailed diagram of the anatomy of the ear adorned the wall.

A resident entered. After asking a few questions, it was apparent this was a new doctor finding his patient manner. He brought up my image on the computer screen. I couldn't wait any longer. "Do you know if I'll have surgery or radiation?"

"It will be surgery for your tumor. It's too large for the other treatment options."

He finished his busywork and left the room. Kayla and I looked at each other.

Dr. Driscoll, the otorhinolaryngologist, came in. He was meticulously dressed in a sharp brown herringbone suit, with coordinated socks. He said it would have to be surgery for my tumor because of the size and location. It was that simple. No other options. I suddenly had no idea what questions to ask. With all my research, I felt good about my understanding. They would use the suboccipital approach, which requires drilling into the skull behind the right ear.

He seemed quite serious, and I later realized that despite our efforts to keep it light with jokes, this was a brain tumor. It couldn't be minimized or wished away. It started sinking in. The doctors at Mayo found Sally Stap's tumor challenging. That wasn't a good sign. There wasn't anything to laugh about. We weren't watching a Discovery Health show about somebody else. This was me.

Always the optimist, I asked, "Given the approach you're proposing, it sounds like my hearing will be retained."

"No, it won't." His answer was simple, short, and direct. Maybe even a bit sad.

Silence filled the room. I inhaled to gain control of my spiraling morale.

Outwardly cheerful, I said, "Well at least I'll get rid of this darn ringing in my ear."

Again, "No, you won't." That same answer. No optimism. "You will most likely lose your hearing and still have ringing. We don't know why that happens, but it usually does."

My emotions started to win and demanded to be felt. My voice was choked, and I was struggling. I swallowed repeatedly. Kayla looked away from me and started talking when she realized I couldn't speak. "What kind of haircut will Mom end up with?"

The doctor laughed for the first time. "We wouldn't be able to make a living as barbers." He showed us on his head the area behind my ear that would be shaved.

Dr. Link, the neurosurgeon, entered next. He was tall, dressed in a navy blue suit, with dark hair and a friendly smile. He was personable and spent a few minutes just talking with us. He repeated what they had recommended for my tumor. He said I would probably have at least some temporary "facial weakness" following the surgery in addition to losing my hearing on the right side. I had no idea exactly what they meant by a weakness. My research had talked about the facial nerve being affected, but again I felt that if I had not lost anything yet, I wouldn't as a result of the surgery. It still wasn't fully sinking in that it was a large and difficult tumor. The actual outcome is always individual, and they just don't know what they will encounter until they get into one's skull.

When asking about recovery time, he predicted I could get back to work at least part time at six weeks. I pointed out that I have to be 100% healthy and my job in consulting required me to travel every week. He immediately revised his prediction to three months. I remember seeing him sitting thoughtfully, looking at the tumor on the screen. "What I worry about with you long term is headaches."

Kayla again asked about my haircut. It was the easy topic that lightened things up. His nurse told us there really isn't much hair shaved.

"Well," I asked, "when can we do it? Let's get it over with." I couldn't think of any further questions. The doctors were nice and I didn't feel rushed at all. I know everyone says to get multiple opinions, but I didn't want to drag this out. I wanted to get the tumor out of me and get it over with. I knew Mayo was the best.

The doctor opened a calendar on the computer, and we agreed on November 3. One of the doctors had jury duty for the last two weeks of October, so we couldn't schedule until November. I told him I had a vacation scheduled for December. He initially suggested we schedule the surgery for after my vacation. Kayla pointed out it was a three-week vacation, by myself, out of the country. I had planned a cruise through the Panama Canal followed by several days in the Galapagos Islands. When the doctor heard three weeks, alone and out of the country, he said I should skip my vacation and he would write a letter for my vacation insurance. We really did need to get that tumor out sooner rather than later. It was compressing my brain stem, which was problematic. Oh boy.

That was it. No more testing. No discussion. No creepy watch and wait. No decisions. There was nothing to laugh at. I had a serious brain tumor that was compressing my brain stem. It had to come out. Right away. By a Mayo Clinic brain surgeon. Jiminy Cricket! Where was God now?

The doctors were patient and unhurried. "Any more questions?"

I shrugged, "I guess not. See you in November!" We really had nothing to add to what, according to the brain surgeons' faces, was a serious medical issue.

Kayla and I went back to our hotel room and collapsed. "A bit stiff, but I like them. I'm comfortable with those two guys getting in my head," I joked.

"Yea, they were great. You have answers, Mom."

I wanted to be done. I wanted to return to my life with minimal disruption. I was concerned about missing so much work. My work ethic was still active and for every day I didn't work, the guilt piled up.

Upon returning to the hotel, I sent a note to all the people on my growing e-mail distribution list.

It was an exhausting but good day. The doctors said I have to have surgery. Radiation is out for the following reasons:

1. I am young, and there is now some evidence radiation could, long term, trigger the remains of the tumor to become malignant.
2. It is very large, and it has pushed quite far into the brain. (Most are closer to the ear; mine grew back into the brain.)
3. If radiation doesn't work, surgery would be very difficult with the scar tissue/tumor that remains.

It was discouraging to hear my hearing will be lost on the right side. They said there will be too much damage done by the removal of the tumor. There is a small chance of some retained hearing, if the planets are aligned right and my anatomy is right when they get in there. There is a 20% chance of facial weakness, but they will make all efforts to minimize damage there.

They seemed amazed I am walking around, pretty normal in most respects. I have had no balance problems—but they think my balance is shot on the right side and my left side has learned to compensate. I saw them looking at me several times, and remarked about my overall functionality.

A Long Weekend

We had to stay over the weekend for a presurgery physical examination on Monday. On Saturday we drove north about an hour to the Mall of America and tried to have fun. We talked about the stores that we were interested in. We studied the mall map. The tumor loomed over us, refusing to be ignored; demanding a voice in every conversation. We walked around and had a nice lunch. I was small, in a bubble of fragility, surrounded by hundreds of stores and thousands of people. I tried to shake it off. I tried to care about any of it. I didn't. I couldn't.

We explored a shoe store and bought matching slippers. I now had new slippers for the hospital. We continued walking, and after passing store after store without entering, we stopped and looked at each other.

"Well, Kayla, do you need anything?"

"No, Mom. And you?"

"No. I guess shopping is a bit silly. What do we need when I have a brain tumor and you don't have a job?" We chuckled. We returned to the car. We returned to Rochester. We returned to Mayo territory.

On Sunday, we bought a comfy athletic set of pants and top for me at Wal-Mart to wear home from the hospital after surgery. We remarked it was sad having the highlight of shopping be slippers for the hospital and a sweat suit for coming home. We went to a movie. Any activity provided distraction.

Monday morning came. I had a meeting with the anesthesiologist. He spent quite a bit of time talking to me, giving me a pep talk. He said I would be up and around in a couple days and I would be back to my old life before I knew it. They found a minor irregularity with my heart, which I had never heard about before and never heard about again. The doctor encouraged me to get in as good a shape as possible before the surgery. He said I should be working out every day and walking a lot. I should be focusing on my heart health. If I needed something to focus on and get ready, exercise was a good way to prepare.

We drove back to Michigan on Monday afternoon, relieved to at least know what the treatment would be. We were discouraged that it was a month out, but it was scheduled. Our ever-present speculation now shifted to the recovery period.

Chapter 5

The Blog Begins

I spent the month of October preparing for brain surgery. *How do you even do that?* I constantly asked myself. Each morning I got on my elliptical machine for half an hour. Many days I would take my dogs over to a nearby preserve to walk. Al Sabo is a land preserve housing the city's water wells. It is covered with woods and meadows with walking paths wound throughout. I had taken the dogs there many times as a respite from my busy life. I found it peaceful and serene. My father would join us frequently during this month of waiting. Our spirits were good, and I talked nonstop about the tumor as we hiked up and down the dips in the woods. We would stop and rest ourselves and the pets at a lookout providing a view of trees, swamps, and ponds.

Spending time with Dad reminded me of how much he had always been available to me through the years. As a young girl, we spent

Sunday afternoons riding our horses on a farm we lived on. Even when I'm sure he could have used some alone time, we saddled up together and headed out. As a teenager, he always set aside whatever he was working on if he heard my light tap on his office door. As a young woman, he was always on the other end of the phone, and quickly at my place with a hammer, drill, or wrench to fix the latest crisis. As a grandfather to my daughters, he would instill values in them for their lifetimes. And once again, in my need, he was there. Listening. Talking. Praying for me.

I didn't feel frightened about the tumor for some reason. If predictions were right, I would recover quickly. My family kept a close eye on me that month. I had a brain tumor! Fortunately, the surgeon's nurse had given me her phone number for questions. So I called to make sure it was okay to get a flu shot. I asked about having my hair highlighted, which I had done for years. She told me I wouldn't be able to do anything to my hair color for three months after surgery. They were minor questions but I wanted to do everything exactly right.

I continued the process of telling friends. I was surprised at the number of people in my life who I wanted to know. I got an absentee ballot for the national presidential election. It was strange to process the fact that I would miss the election due to brain surgery!

Nancy, a friend in Florida, mailed me packages to lift my spirits. She sent me a pair of shoes with a plaque saying, "The best way to forget all your troubles is to wear tight shoes." She later sent me a Raquel Welch wig, and then a Hannah Montana wig. We laughed on the phone when I'd open a package.

I continued my house cleaning projects. I bagged up extra clothes and dropped them at Goodwill. I walked my dogs in the neighborhood and nearby woods.

It was during this period before we went to Mayo Clinic that I started a blog. The e-mail distribution list with all the people who needed to be updated continued to grow. I sent an e-mail to all the people on the list with the URL for the blog. How do you start a blog with the subject of "brain tumor removal?" Well, I decided to take the educational approach. So I started with the story of what happened to me and how I had learned about the tumor. I started a FAQ section to answer questions people would have. I wanted people to see my faith speaking through the blog gently. I included what people could do, because they had asked. All they could do was pray. I wanted to take advantage of every prayer offer available. So I gave them what to pray for in simple and complex versions. Once I sent out the URL, I received a lot of comments. I promised Kayla would be updating it through my surgery to keep everyone posted. That would make it easy for Kayla to update one place and not have a lot of people to e-mail or call. People loved the idea. Amazingly, word spread. I heard from people over the next month who I hadn't talked to for years.

I populated the blog with pictures of the Mayo Clinic area, as well as pictures from my walks of autumn colors and nature. Brain tumor surgery was frustrating to prepare for. I took the blog on like an IT project. It was something I could do. Just a few days before heading back to Mayo, I sent a note to tell everyone where to look for updates:

October 28, 2008
Greetings to all,
I have set up a blog to provide updates on my progress over the next few months. I started with two sections—a FAQ section, and a section on what you can do (hint? Pray a lot).
http://mybigmayoadventure.blogspot.com/

I decided to set up a blog rather than use Mayo's CarePages for your convenience. With this blog, you don't have to login to check status. You can leave comments if you like, and I approved anonymous comments so people don't have to set up ids in Google. However, PLEASE remember to put your name in those comments so I know who "stopped by" my blog.

I appreciate everyone's support through this challenging time. This week I'm keeping myself busy with errands and busy work. I'll leave Sunday for surgery at Mayo Clinic (St Mary's Hospital) on Monday. I hope to be back home about a week later.

Kayla will update the blog starting Monday while I'm offline. We won't send e-mail. However, I will read any notes you send when I can. (Which you can guess will be as soon as they let me have my laptop or Blackberry.)

More to come. . .

Sally

p.s. Feel free to pass this on to anyone who you don't think I included. (Even though the list is bcc'd ☺)

October 28, 2008

What can you do?

Everyone wants to know what they can do to help. I have been overwhelmed by everyone's concern and notes—seriously. One thing you can do is keep those notes coming. I will need them post-surgery to keep my spirits up. Kayla will be posting updates to this blog, and will read any posted comments to me until I am back online again. (Please sign your name to comments posted to this blog if you use the anonymous option!!)

Many of you have offered to pray for me and have asked what to pray for. Well, as it turns out, unless anyone can take my place at Mayo, it appears prayer is just about all you can do to help at this point.

I accept all prayer offers!! He is listening....

Here's what you can pray for. I have included a simple prayer for beginners. I have also provided complex and specific detail for prayer warriors.

Option One:

Simple

"Dear God, Please help Sally get through this and have a full recovery."

Option Two:

Complex and Specific

This week

I need to stay healthy and not get any colds or flu.

I need to stay sane.

Sunday (November 2)

Safe travels on the 8 hour drive to Rochester MN (Kayla, Dad, Al, and I).

I hope to get some sleep on Sunday night before the early surgery on Monday.

Monday (November 3)

Successful surgery at St Mary's Hospital in Rochester (full day of surgery).

Pray for the surgeons and the surgical team.

The surgeons prefer the tumor come away from healthy tissues easily (not sticky—the technical term they used).

We want the nerves left intact following the tumor removal (facial muscles, facial sensation, and hearing).

No spinal fluid leak following surgery (they need to get the skull sealed well).

No impact to my brain stem which is pretty necessary for life.

Of course, we want full removal of the tumor.

My family will be hanging out for a long day and need patience (I have the easy part that day—stay unconscious).

Postsurgery (Monday night and beyond)

Minimal pain (there is a limit to pain med allowed so they can determine how I am doing without having any issues masked by drugs).

That I will quickly regain balance (the docs say my right balance is gone and has been picked up by the left side. We hope that means balance won't be a big issue if that transition has already taken place).

Minimal or NO facial nerve impact. There is a forecast of some facial muscle "weakening" that I should regain soon after surgery.

The forecast is no remaining hearing on the right side. However, at least some hearing preservation would be greatly appreciated by me even though it is a long shot.

Reduced ringing in the ears. While it seems illogical, even though I will lose hearing, there is a high likelihood I will still hear ringing. Go figure....

I will have to learn patience and to accept help while recovering. I predict this will be my biggest challenge.

Comments

"Hi Sally … awesome blog site!! Thanks for a great explanation of what is going on. Aren't you glad that you are at a 'young' age so that you will heal quicker!! :) … We are praying for a successful day on the 3rd and that your recovery will be uneventful. Be assured that you are being attended to by the Great Physician. He has nothing but good things in store for you."

"I encourage you to be peaceful, if for no other reason than it doesn't do any good for you not to be. You have done the very best you can to get the very best medical care you can, at a very good institution. You are fortunate to have a very helpful family (both upwards to your parents and downwards to your children) to support you in this. So just as when you get on an airplane, there reaches a point where you just have to trust that you have a competent pilot and just turn over your fate to him or her, when you go into surgery be peaceful and understand that you will have very good care, and we'll see you when you come out of it."

Kayla—You are a great daughter and we are all so thankful Sally has you by her side. I know Kendra would be there also if she wasn't so far away, so our thoughts are with her too. I'm sure it's very hard for her to be separated from her mom and sister right now.

Chapter 6

Final Prep

veryone in my life worried about my non-stop research. I wasn't to be deterred though as it educated me. I found it might not be as easy as everyone was predicting—or at least telling me. In hindsight though, I was educated but naïve. I discounted anything scary. I read about facial weakness and learned it was a term used for paralysis, i.e., no movement on the face. I read about gold weights people had implanted in their eyelids that wouldn't close. I shuddered. Poor souls. I read about debilitating headaches that crippled people. It was scary. I just couldn't believe I would have one of those outcomes. None of those things would happen to me because I was too busy and couldn't take much time off. Some of the effects reported just sounded awful, and I couldn't go out in public that way! My God would never allow me to go through that! This research would prove invaluable, tidbits in memory, to tap into throughout my recovery.

The last week before surgery arrived, and I went to lunch and dinner one more time with friends. I had my last haircut. My dog Paulo graduated from his obedience class due to some extra sessions our instructor held for us. Mary, a friend in my Bible study group who was a massage therapist, offered to give me a free massage as a send-off. It was great for my stressed body, and I was touched by her generosity. I was humbled by the concern everyone expressed in my life. I was starting to learn that accepting help was actually kind of neat.

Where was God? I felt God through the support of my family and friends as I prepared for Mayo Clinic. I felt compassion in the members of my Bible Study group as they prayed for me. I prayed for healing. I prayed for minimal pain. I prayed for an excellent outcome. I prayed to beat the odds. I prayed for a miracle.

Once I had started the blog, I wanted to update it regularly. Prior to surgery, there wasn't much. However, I was determined to entertain anyone who took the time to check in with the blog.

October 29, 2008

BTEP

Today something a bit silly. . .

As you know, my background is computer science and I've spent my career in Information Technology management, surrounded by acronyms for projects and systems. I think we need an acronym for this project. Therefore, today I am announcing the launch of the BTEP: Brain Tumor Eradication Project. For non-IT folks, acronyms can be either pronounced or spelled. So it is perfectly acceptable to say "B.T.E.P.", or to say B-TEP. There are some acronyms in the world that are picky, like SAS (say it SAS,) or SAP (Say it S.A.P) ... But since this is my acronym, I say either is fine.

Yesterday's BTEP Milestone? Haircut. You may ask yourself. . . "She has a brain tumor and she's worried about her hair?" Well, yes. There are some really big issues here that I have no control over. But my hair? That I can have some control over. The surgery will require not a full shave … inhale, exhale, sigh of relief! But there will be a patch behind my right ear that will be shaved. No idea how much.

So after much analysis (there are downsides to being so analytical,) speculation of the diameter of the target bald patch, and consultation with a professional (Kris at Folio in Kalamazoo), we decided to stick with longer hair to hopefully cover the still undefined bald spot, and to go with lowlights (i.e., darker hair) to minimize root growth for the three recovery months that I cannot do anything to my head. After all, a girl has to feel good about her hair before going into brain surgery, right?

The countdown continues … and you can now see why I included a prayer request for this week to help me maintain my sanity. :)

Have a Happy Wednesday!!!!

p.s. Kayla—I sure hope you are gearing up to be this entertaining with my surgery updates. :)

Comments

Kayla said … If I ever wonder where I got the trait to over-analyze absolutely everything, I will just re-read this post and know! At any rate, I will try my best to be as entertaining as you … after all, I have learned from the best, but cannot promise anything. Happy Thursday!

The day before we left for surgery, I went to a church meeting to see some Freedom in Christ ministry people who were in town. I was asked to say something about my surgery. I was nervous and shook as I described my upcoming event. There were only a few people who I knew, but when they asked anyone interested to come pray over me, almost everyone rose from their seats and came forward. They laid their hands on me and prayed. They prayed generally for my health and surgery. They prayed specifically that the tumor not be sticky, meaning tightly adhered to my healthy tissues, and it be easily removed. I thought I had my bases covered. Why would God not answer the prayers of His devoted followers? However, when I listened for God's voice, I heard little back. Possibly, "I'm with you, my child." Evidently, this wasn't going to be easy. I shook it off.

I cleaned my house. I had my "affairs in order." The night before leaving, I stared at my bedroom's tray ceiling, tracing lines around the room. This was unbelievable. Sleep escaped me, and I tossed and turned. I couldn't clear my head. I welcomed morning and was ready to leave. I was conflicted of course, as what I was heading toward was going to be the biggest challenge of my life. One foot in front of the other.

Chapter 7

Heading into the Fire

My entourage headed to Rochester, Minnesota, on November 2, 2008. It had been decided Al, Dad, and Kayla would go with me to Mayo for the surgery. My mother would stay with my pets in Michigan, with promised frequent updates. I felt embraced and loved by my family.

As Al only planned to stay for the day of surgery and maybe a little longer, we took two cars. He was my chauffeur, with Kayla and Dad following in the second car. We talked between cars over walkie-talkies and shared laughs as we stopped for food. We joked about turning around. We joked about heading into a firing squad. We joked about anything possible to keep from facing the truth.

My family didn't want me to drive so I could be well rested for surgery the next day. I pointed out that I would be sleeping all day; it was probably them that needed rest. I was the queen of the day, the center of attention. Attention I was reluctant to have, that felt sticky. I chose when we stopped, where we ate. I remember stopping at a rest area, asking for just a couple more minutes. I stood outside the car and inhaled the unseasonably warm air. I was taking in the barren fall trees and blue sky while grasping the phrase "drink in your surroundings" with a new understanding.

November 2, 2008
Welcome to Rochester
STATUS: I will be reporting to the hospital at 6 AM CST Monday AM for admission and surgery prep. Kayla will take over updates for me until?? I really can't think of anything witty to say at this point. Scared? Yep. Appreciative? Sure am. Strong faith in God? Absolutely. I hope to be back online soon!!

==========

The caravan arrived in Rochester, MN this afternoon around 3 PM CST. This gave plenty of time for a quick walking tour for, believe it or not, more speculation about where I will specifically be in the massive hospital tomorrow for surgery and afterwards for recovery. The drive went well and despite the clouds, I snapped a few pictures while driving and upon arrival here in Rochester.

St Mary's is HUGE.

The Patient—Before. . .

Home away from home in
Rochester for Kayla, Dad, Al

Oh, and here's the Sears
Tower as we sped by on I-94.

We arrived in Rochester late afternoon. I had made reservations at a hotel across the street from the hospital so my family would be able to go back and forth as needed. We walked around the hospital to know where to go the next day. I excitedly pointed out features of the hospital. I took pictures for my blog.

It was a beautiful 70-degree Indian summer day, and we sat outside for a long time. The four of us lined up awkwardly in chairs outside the hotel in their offseason patio area. Pain etched on my family's faces as they tried to enjoy their time with me as the clock ticked down. We had a one-hour time difference as well as the switch from daylight saving time that weekend. So our bodies thought it was two hours later than the clock.

We headed to dinner early, stretching all activities to keep busy. The Canadian Honker is a family restaurant near the hotel, so we walked. I ordered food but ate little of the large portions served. I had no taste for food. I was running out of things to talk about.

We were tired, but I had to stay awake until nine to call a phone number to find out when to report to the hospital the next day. We watched the clock, willing it to move faster. Finally, I learned I was to report to the hospital at six AM. We headed to our respective rooms. I turned over control of the blog to Kayla. She and I were in one room and Al and Dad were next door. I don't know if anyone slept well that night. I was awake by three o'clock. I took a shower about four o'clock. We headed to the hospital at 5:30. I couldn't eat prior to surgery, but my family was hungry. They tried to sneak a donut from the hotel dining area even though it hadn't opened. They were chastised by the woman working there. We laughed. Again.

Chapter 8

Mayo Days:
Monday

Under the Knife

There were a lot of people already in line at the reception area at 5:45 AM. I was still in denial. I was a little too cheerful. I knew my family had a long day ahead of them. I anticipated when I awoke from surgery my life would be different. I was antsy. I wanted to get to the unconscious part.

Mayo Clinic is huge and well organized. You rarely spend much time waiting. The same is true for surgery. After checking into the reception area and sitting for a few minutes, we were escorted to the surgery area. Everyone was too quiet. I started joking with my family about where we would eat dinner that night. Even though we knew I wouldn't be having dinner that night or anytime soon, I talked about the options and acted like all would be normal again. I was taken to a changing/examining room. My family stepped out while I changed into hospital garb. It started to feel real. The nurse took my history. I hadn't had surgery other than caesareans many years before. The nurse escorted my family back in where we waited. Not much time went by before another escort came to take me to surgery.

We were all choked up as I left. I did my best to smile as I hugged them and said goodbye. The thought of

Lesson Learned
It will hurt. It will also get better even if it's not the same as before.

dying didn't really spend much time in my consciousness. I did believe I would see them. I just didn't know how I would look or feel when I saw them next. The nurse and I walked to the recovery area, where I was shown my gurney and prepared for surgery. I watched people coming and going around me, as I lay fidgeting. I couldn't get comfortable. I prayed. I heard nothing back.

I was asked several times to say my name and date of birth. The surgical team came in and marked my head with the surgeon's initials where they were going to drill. That reassured me they would be drilling in the correct side of my brain. I prayed. Eventually it was my turn.

The assistant anesthesiologist wheeled me into the operating room on a gurney. I was calm. We turned down a hall lined with room after room with scrubbing sinks. That was a lot of operating rooms. I saw Dr. Link walking in the hallway with his hands behind his back. "Hey doc, I've got lunch plans so let's get this thing over with." I tapped my wrist where I normally wore a watch.

He smiled, "These things can be rushed if you really wish…."

I quickly answered, "Oh no, take your time!!" What I really wanted to say was that I was a person, and hoped they remembered that while drilling, removing the tumor, and closing me up. I wanted to be *me* when I woke up.

I couldn't wait for them to finish putting an IV into my hand so they would put me under. I just wanted to be unconscious. The surgical room was busy and efficiently noisy. I heard tinny rattling of many instruments on trays on one side of the room. Instruments for an eight-hour surgery. People hurried around the room, each focused on a task. The assistant anesthesiologist put my first IV in.

A commanding voice was in the background telling people how he wanted the operating room arranged, "Move that over here, move that over there." I was reassured by his confidence. I gulped when he added, "Because if we need to resuscitate we need this area clear."

Oh my. I guess the anesthesiologist knows what he's doing.

A nurse leaned in to tell me the operating room was dedicated to acoustic neuroma surgeries. *Scary that so many people go through this.* She told me she would be massaging the side I was laying on every hour. *I never thought of that.* It was reassuring because I would be laying on it for all-day surgery.

I told her there were a lot of people praying for the surgical team that day. I noticed a guy standing in the background to observe. He was clearly ensuring that he wasn't in the way. The Mayo line of command was clear.

Someone said something about a nap. I looked at the bright lights, *I have to remember this.* Then I was out because I remember nothing until I woke up that night. After I was asleep the surgical team had a field day. Here's what I know about:

IVs: They started a second IV in my right hand. And they started "arterial" IVs in each wrist. So I woke up with four IVs. I think the arterial IV was used to measure my blood gasses.

Blood pressure cuff: put on my right arm, and it was automatic all day.

Calf compression: I had put on compression socks that morning, but they added something to each leg to inflate and deflate automatically to keep the blood flowing. I was stuck with them for several days.

Catheter: self-explanatory.

Monitors: They wired up my face and neck. The nerves were stimulated regularly through the day to see if the signal was still flowing. The monitors were gone when I woke up.

Bolted head: They bolted my head into a vice-like frame to ensure nothing moved. That was gone when I woke up, but it left three small spots that have since healed.

November 3, 2008

Surgery Day (by Kayla)

After an uneventful night in Mom's and my room, we found out on the other side of the wall (aka Grandpa's and Al's room) there was a bit more excitement throughout the night. First, the battery in the smoke detector blew up - sounding like a gunshot and waking them both. Second, the light between the beds came on all by itself and caused them both to stare at one another wondering what the other was thinking turning on the light like that. Finally, after a night like that, what do you want? - A nice cup of coffee ... and what do you know, the coffee maker doesn't work.

On to the serious stuff....

3:30 AM - Yes, you guessed—we were up. Mom got a few hours of sleep before waking up at 3:30am CST. It really didn't help that the time just changed and we are in a different time zone.

5:45 AM - We reported to the hospital lobby and got in the long line to check-in/register.

6:00 AM - Escorted upstairs to the pre-prep room for a quick review of her health history and a double check of her name and date of birth (for the third time this morning).

7:00 AM - The escort arrived to take her away to the prep room where she will get her IV and such to prep for surgery. This is expected to be around a two-hour process by the time they get all of the sensors connected to monitor the critical nerves in the body. Grandpa, Al, and I are now doing our best to wait patiently in the surgical waiting room.

8:17 AM - She entered the OR. At 9:15 am someone came to tell us she was asleep and the final preparations for surgery were underway.

9:18 AM - Surgery began. We will be updated in a couple of hours on her progress.

10:15 AM - We went out to lunch. It was little early, but after getting up at 3:30 in the morning we were ready for some food. Last night we went to the Canadian Honker for dinner and it was such a hit we decided to have lunch there—after all, we do have a little time on our hands. And while some would wonder at the name, the food is excellent.

11:45 AM - We have been moved from the 2nd floor waiting room to the ICU waiting room on the 8th floor. No real update on surgery, except that it will be "hours" which is something we already knew. The waiting continues.

12:15 PM - Nap time for Grandpa, Al, and myself.

1:00 PM - Phone rings in the waiting room with an update ... we all wake up. She is doing very well. Once again we were told to get something to eat if we are hungry and they would contact us again in a couple of hours with an update.

2:45 PM - She is doing very well. Our surgical communicator said it shouldn't be too much longer - meaning it could be less than 2 hours at this point, but she didn't want to commit to a definite time.

3:20 PM - A different surgical communicator came to visit us after relieving the previous surgical communicator. She indicated that 2 hours, at this point, is optimistic. However, she did say that we will be meeting both surgeons after Mom is moved to recovery (hopefully around 5:30—again optimistic). From that time, Mom will be in recovery for at least one hour before being moved to the ICU. Once in the ICU, it will take 15–20 minutes to get her situated and the monitors connected before we will be allowed to see her.

4:50 PM - The surgeons are closing and they should be ready to meet with us in about 30 minutes.

5:40 PM - The surgical coordinator came to get us to meet with the surgeons. Mom is in recovery and we will see her in a couple of hours.

5:45 PM - Grandpa, Al, and myself met with surgeons. ...

She made it through the surgery well. She will not have any hearing in her right ear. The surgeons said the tumor was very "sticky" to the brain, brain-stem, and facial nerve. Only time will tell.

9:00 PM - We finally got to see her. She is in ICU for the night and doing extremely well according to her nurse. She was talking to us and her sense of humor was already coming through! Now ... sleep for all of us.

Comments

Sally, my prayers are with you this morning. Praying that God will provide the surgeons with supernatural wisdom that the surgery will be 100% successful, and that you and your family will be blanketed with the peace that only He can provide. God Bless.

Thanks, Kayla. Exciting night for the boys!! I wonder if Ghost Hunters knows about that room in your hotel. I am glad you had something to talk about this morning other than the surgery. I'll be checking back all day, and praying all day (complex and specific)!

Thank you, Kayla. I have been praying already this morning, and appreciate the updates. I will check for updates. It's only 8 there now so she is still being prepped, I'm sure. I will stay in touch. Thanks again.

Awesome updates—makes us feel like we are in on what's going on instead of just praying and waiting on pins and needles. Thanks!

It's almost 7 PM here on the east coast, and I have been thinking about you and your family all day. I pray the surgery was a grand success and you can have a restful and healing night. (Including your Dad and Al—Kayla your post about their night was great.) And although I know you would love to have Paulo under the sheets suction-cupped to your leg and Gina snuggled up next to you, I don't think the doctors would appreciate Gabby sitting on your head. A little humor at this anxious time—I pray everything went well.

Thanks God surgery went well, and special thanks to you, Kayla, for keeping us updated. I will continue to pray, and I am sure you're looking forward to talking with her when she's awake (and of course you'll tell us when you do!) Sally—I love you and I miss you! I can't wait to talk with you, and to tell you what a great idea this blog is! Kayla is doing a wonderful job!

Kayla, thank you for taking the time to let us know how everything went today—we all (I know I was not the only one) were waiting for each posting with—well, maybe I now know what "bated breath" means! We love your mom and are keeping her in our prayers as well as the rest of your family.

One day at a time. This was a big day to get behind you. Sounds like it went as well as we could all hope. We'll keep the prayer machine going!

I woke up in the recovery room. The first sensation I had was extreme back pain, followed by my left side hurting, hard as a rock. I wondered about my head, and then it hit me like a vice, squeezing more with each breath. Lying on one side motionless all day during surgery had caused incredible side and back pain. The nurse was behind my head, aware of each movement. She anticipated each need before I could express it.

I couldn't believe it was over. No trips to heaven while unconscious. No hovering over the surgical team. Just the absence of a day of my life. I thought of my family and wondered how they were doing and what they been told. I felt like myself inside. Slowly the realization came over me that some things were not the way they were when I went to sleep. My mouth and eye were not working. I was numbed by narcotics, which stripped away emotion. I was sadly aware though, bit by bit, that things weren't working right. It had to be temporary.

I took inventory of my equipment hookups. A blood pressure cuff intermittently pinched my arm, 4 IVs immobilized my arms, an oxygen tube pricked my nostrils, and a clip on my finger registered my oxygen level. My legs were held captive by compression wraps and a machine that sounded like a heart lung machine inhaling and exhaling.

My nurse called the ICU to let them know I was ready to be moved. She injected pain medication into my IV, assuring me I could have more once moved to the ICU. A transport person came and wheeled me there. I closed my eyes.

Ready to See My Family

The nurses cleaned me up, two on each side. They were gentle while efficient. My family was running out of patience. It was almost nine PM, over fourteen hours since we had said goodbye. It was clear that cleanup was mandatory to ensure that before anyone saw me all of the surgical debris had been removed. I was a mess.

My family weighed on my mind, even in my misery, knowing they had held vigil through a long day. I welcomed their arrival. It brought comfort and connection. It was important to me to reach from my altered state and let them know it was still ME inside. Since we had been joking that morning about having dinner together at the Canadian Honker, the first thing I said, while laying all wired up and immobile, was "I won't make dinner tonight." At first Kayla looked confused, maybe worried, but then she realized I was eking out a joke after nine-plus hours of surgery. I was satisfied that they knew I was okay, but was disappointed I hadn't evoked more laughter.

Al analyzed every monitor they had on me until he was satisfied his little sister was okay. I talked a bit but it was hard and exhausting. My right eye really bothered me and was best left closed. I listened to their murmurs at the foot of the bed, wishing I could join the conversation. My body didn't agree.

After a while, my family left for the night to get some rest. They stopped outside my room and talked to the nurse. They were at a loss about what to do. They were exhausted but didn't know if they should leave me alone. The nurse reassured them she would be watching me closely all night. She took Kayla's cell phone number and promised to call if they were needed. She told them to get some rest and to take care of themselves so they would be able to help me when I needed them most—in the coming days.

I was alone with my pain and thoughts, in the ICU. It was the longest night of my life as I watched the clock advance minute by minute. I couldn't move body parts that felt cemented to the bed. I had no courage or ability to lift my bandage-laden head from the pillow. The pain had been expected but was harder in reality than it had been in theory. I hoped it was within the normal range for this type of surgery. My eye and mouth scared me. Having facial paralysis was one of the most terrifying issues I could think of. Disappointment struck when it registered that God hadn't answered the prayers raised on my behalf. I had hoped for a great outcome I could credit to God and prayers. Maybe it would still happen? I didn't know how temporary my paralysis would be.

The nurse sensed my every need. Despite her regular rearranging of pillows under my back, along my side, and behind my elevated head, I couldn't get comfortable. I entered a cycle of falling asleep and then awakening to see five minutes had passed on the clock. My family said they would be back in the morning by the time the doctor came in at 6:30 AM. In my confusion I saw it was 11:45 and couldn't figure out why nobody had been in yet. I figured out finally that it was PM and they had only been gone for a couple of hours. I didn't want to oversleep and miss the doctors' visit, so my confused mind kept me awake.

The Report

Morning came, and my family arrived around six. The doctors came in shortly after to talk about the surgery. They were pleased the tumor had been fully removed. They asked me questions to check my mental alertness. They checked my leg strength and reflexes. They asked if I had any fluid in my right ear, nose, or down my throat. Leakage of spinal fluid is a frequent complication. Fortunately, that wasn't the case with me. I showed no sign of bleeding in my brain. I shuddered internally at the possibility of any more going wrong.

Cranial nerves are numbered. I was becoming familiar with the nerves being referred to numerically, but I can't say I ever got them straight. The seventh nerve is the facial nerve, which shares a tight space with the eighth nerve, which is the acoustic, or hearing, nerve. The tumor grew on the acoustic nerve. The doctors explained that my facial nerve had slowly changed from a round tube of fibers to a ribbon stretched over the expanding tumor. As they slowly picked the tumor from my facial nerve, it became damaged and ultimately shut down entirely. Wow.

The good news was that my trigeminal nerve, number five, had not been damaged. The facial nerve provides movement and the trigeminal nerve provides feeling. A strange metallic taste in my mouth was hopefully just an angry, but not damaged, nerve.

Healing of a damaged facial nerve is possible but must regrow from inside the brain all the way out to the ends. Due to the length of the nerve fibers, it would take months. An estimated regrowth rate is 1 mm per day. Given that, it would be six months before I would have movement. If it returned. On the bright side, if damage was minimal, it would be sooner.

I thought I was hearing on the right side as I could hear normal sounds in the room and had ringing in my right ear. After asking about it, Dr. Driscoll said, "No, you aren't hearing." Kayla tells me I had been told my hearing was definitely gone but I don't recall ever being told the auditory nerve had actually been removed. When I read that phrase in the surgical notes months later, I had aha moment and said, "Okay, it is gone." Prior to that point I still believed that even though the doctors had said it was gone, I trusted my body could have unexplained healing. Lying in bed at Mayo, I hadn't put all of this together yet.

I shrugged, "Ok." I was hoping to prove him wrong. I didn't know yet the auditory nerve had actually been removed from my head. He told me but my brain didn't hear him.

The tumor had been sticky and vascular (bloody). It was difficult to remove. I asked one doctor about my face. He said they had lost the facial nerve response right at the end of surgery. I asked how long it was going to be before it recovered. They said we would just have to see how much and how soon it came back. He said it would probably be a long wait with less improvement than I wanted. It would never be normal again. Wow. That was a lot to digest.

The doctors suggested I have a "gold" weight implanted in my right upper eyelid. Gold weights are actually made of titanium. Evidently when they were made of gold, they were frequently stolen because of the value of gold. Also, many people had allergies to the metal. I did have the ability to partially close my eye, but my natural ability to blink frequently was gone. For the health of my cornea, I had to keep it lubricated. Fortunately, the ability to open my eye was not affected. It was interesting to me as it was one of the last things I had learned while doing research. It sounded crazy when I read about it. And now, it was being recommended for me. Some of the people who I had read about had gold weights implanted quite some time after their surgeries. So this was good news that they were going to add it before I had problems with my eye. But it was really bad news because it meant my eye and face would not be working for quite some time.

Once again, it occurred to me that this would be disappointing for the people who had been praying specifically that it be easy to remove and there would be minimal facial nerve damage. How disappointing, as I had wanted to point out to everyone how great God was and how He answered prayers. How embarrassing it was going to be when I returned to work. How could I interact with clients? Smiling was such a big part of who I was. And now I would also have a weighted eyelid! Maybe my facial movement would be back by the end of my planned three-month furlough. Then again, I was guessing that doctors didn't slice into an eyelid for a short-term fix.

A resident came in with what looked like a fishing tackle box. She taped eye weights onto my eyelid in order to determine what weight I needed. After going back and forth a bit, she decided on a weight that was more than ideal but a bit light for what my eye needed. She suggested that it was a balance of getting the eye to close but not weighting it too heavily. I hoped that she was right with the weight chosen. I was disappointed that it wasn't the lightest weight possible.

Pain was overwhelming. It took every bit of energy just to hang on. Every bit of everything to just be. Every bit of control to not scream. Every bit of strength to not give up. I felt trapped. I felt angry. I was scared. I couldn't cry. At one point in the morning, only my brother and a nurse were in the room with me. I got sick suddenly and violently. A female administrator who was walking down the hall must have heard something and she immediately stepped in the room, leaving paperwork by the door, and started to help. When I lifted my head and opened my eyes, there were three nurses in the room. Once things were under control, the administrator sanitized, picked up her paperwork, and continued on. Once again I was impressed by the compassion and efficiency of the hospital staff. My brother, without blinking, replaced my blanket after I expressed concern that I was getting the blanket soiled. "No problem. This is the easy part."

Where was God? He was providing support through the love of my family, skill of the nursing staff, the incredible skill of the brain surgeon. But why hadn't He answered my prayers? Why did I have to suffer so much? Where was He in my pain? I was so confused. I was terrified. This wasn't a cute testimony. Would it really be better in a few days as predicted?

Chapter 9

Mayo Days: Tuesday

Progress and Support

November 4, 2008

The Day After (by Kayla)

Mom is doing very well this morning. She was able to get as much rest last night as possible considering she is in the ICU and they woke her up every half hour or so. Both of her surgeons stopped by this morning for a quick check-up and their interns came earlier for a more thorough evaluation.

She is struggling a bit with dizziness, nausea, and pain. These are common issues with acoustic neuroma patients. They are giving her meds to help with that and so far she has been able to keep the pain pills down. She will be moved to a regular room later today.

10:30 AM - Mom was just moved into a regular room on a neurological floor. The move went well and she made it up to the next floor with minimal nausea. She is in Room #9-714 in the Mary Brigh building. She has a great view of the helicopter pad from her room. This will be her room until she is ready to head back home. Two bites of Jell-O she tried went down well!

1:00 PM (From Sally) - This is boring, because I can't move without nausea setting in! My brain is still in here and functioning. Kayla is reading the comments to me—thank you so much for all the encouraging words!

5:30 PM - One clarification from earlier ... Mom was not actually on the computer, but asked me to write a quick note to everyone for her. She is still struggling with pain and nausea. I will be spending the night with her tonight, since she is on a regular floor with less monitoring and we anticipate a bit of a rough night.

Comments

I am so relieved to hear all the progress and good news. One day at a time, one Jell-O bite at a time. Kayla thank you so much for keeping us all informed.

Thanks for taking the time to keep us informed. I am glad to hear Sally is doing well!

This is such a cool way to keep all informed. How will we update the pets? I hope you guys get some rest.

Does anyone else see the hospital humor of them putting someone with hearing loss near the helicopter pad?

Kayla has done a great job of keeping the world up to date on your status. Like everyone else, I'm incredibly happy to know that this is behind you. Enjoy the boredom!

Why am I not surprised that you are bored already? I'm so grateful that Kayla has kept us up-to-date on your progress yesterday and today. I am looking forward to more good reports coming out of Rochester. So ... how big is the bald patch? Take care. We love you.

We should have known we'd be hearing from you less than 24 hours after having major surgery! You're quite the trooper! Hang in there and enjoy the boredom. You'll be back among the working in no time.

I'm so glad you are staying tonight Kayla. I'm sure it's a great comfort to your mom. Hang in there Sally with a few rough days and soon you'll be walking through Al Sabo again.

Mid-morning on Tuesday, I was moved from the ICU to the neurological floor. The ride was bright, even through my closed eyelids. I felt hospital air flowing over me with the smells of drugs and sickness. I was surrounded by noises of people, the calming voice of the transport person who took care with every bump and the occasional squeak or groan of my hospital bed. The elevator seemed strange and foreign as I lay horizontal, peeking up at the ceiling. I clung to my blankets. I wasn't sure if I was ready to "graduate" from the ICU.

My room was large and bright. The window opened onto a cold and snowy day as the temperature had dropped and it snowed overnight. I was told I was overlooking the helicopter pad. One colleague later joked that putting the newly single-sided deaf lady by the noisy pad was ironic. Equipment was behind me, and my view straight ahead was a whiteboard with the nurses' names and the date.

The floor nurses hustled in quickly to evaluate their new charge. Everyone was friendly, supportive, and cheerful. They acted hopeful. I numbly watched people scurry around the room. My family interacted with them as they settled in for what they knew to be their home away from home for the next few days.

Over the following hours, I was slowly unplugged from equipment, like plucking petals from a daisy. First the heart monitor went silent.

I hoped my heart was strong enough to carry me through this ordeal. Then the annoying oxygen hose from my nostrils. I was happy to lose the drying air and tubes that kept falling from behind my ears. This was followed by the oxygen clamp on one finger. What relief I felt when they removed arterial IVs out of each wrist. With each disconnection, I was one step closer to independence. That left two IV lines for fluids and antibiotics flowing into my body and the not so discreet urinary catheter catching the output. Oh, and then there was a compression contraption on my legs, limiting their mobility and pumping my calves with huffing inflation sounds followed by a hissing release of air as it deflated. And of course, there was the huge white bandage surrounding my immobile head.

The pain and discomfort were constant. I didn't want to move, as I would become nauseous immediately. I took in so much air every time I tried to swallow pills I would vomit after getting them down. My left side was incredibly painful with bursts of fire with each move. My head hurt in a way no word exists to describe. My eye was dry unless constantly lubricated. I had no idea how I was ever going to get out of bed. I was grateful they didn't push me to get up. I was even more grateful that there was no mention of removing my catheter.

It was extremely helpful to have Kayla, Dad, and Al there all the time as my advocate to ensure I had my meds, food, anything I needed. The nurses were attentive, but there was always something additional my family added to my care. We had joked prior to the surgery about having Kayla feed me ice chips. Well, in the hospital it was no joke. There was nothing that hit the spot for me like ice chips melting on my always parched tongue. The nurses showed her where she could get towels, sheets, water, and ice chips, and where she could store items in the freezer. I didn't want to disappoint her by being weak or by not recovering. I was scared. I never said it.

The nurses brought a cot for Kayla so she could spend nights in my room. As I watched her set up her cot for the night, I remembered her hospital stay at age thirteen. She had her appendix out, and I insisted on staying in her room. I remembered setting up my own cot and the value of my stay. She needed her mother with her, and I was able to avert problems. In the middle of the night, she urgently needed red Jell-O, not green, and I was able to work with the nurses to find some. We had chuckled for years about the urgency of "not green Jell-O." Now she was here, setting up to see to my needs. Exactly when had the switch in parent-child roles happened?

Kayla read blog comments to me. Listening to them was overwhelming to me. Some were heartfelt. Some were funny. Through all of them I could hear relief. That, right then, was the beginning of my "conflict of authenticity." Everyone was so excited about being through with brain surgery. I wasn't feeling relief. The pain and challenges kept me captive, and I wondered at the gap between everyone's excitement and my misery. It was like struggling to not drown. I could never let my guard down. I could never rest or relax. Everyone was relieved I was alive, not expecting me to survive surgery. I wasn't sure I had.

Despite my pain, I couldn't believe how many people were reaching out to me. The blog was a great success. It gave Kayla something helpful to do, and we got almost immediate encouraging feedback. People had the blog up on their desktops at home and work. I told Kayla what to post for me. I thanked all the friends and family who had taken the time to keep checking in on me. I said I was bored, but I think it would have been more accurate to say I was overwhelmed and drowning.

Every morning and night my team of doctors visited me. It included Dr. Link, Dr. Driscoll, and several residents. It was evident the team would discuss and strategize after each visit. I was a learning opportunity for the residents. The morning after telling Dr. Driscoll I thought I could hear on the right side, the team entered enthusiastically, and asked me to listen to the phone. Dr. Driscoll picked up the room phone, held the phone up to my left ear and asked if I could hear it. Yes, I could hear a loud dial tone. He then held the phone on my right side. Nothing. I heard nothing. "I guess you guys were right, I hear nothing." That was blunt, but demonstrated that I clearly had no hearing remaining on the right side.

The day continued with struggles including head pain, a dry eye, and struggling to keep food and pills down. The nurses brought a plastic bubble that was taped to my face, covering my dry eye to conserve moisture. Hourly they would put eye drops in. We tracked each dose of pain meds and asked for more whenever the window opened again. Swallowing was difficult, and I would take in too much air, leading to throwing it all up again soon after.

Food tasted wrong. Pepsi sounded really good and then tasted like tinfoil. The nurse explained that taste is affected by the surgery. Exhausted, I settled in for another night, hoping for longer stretches of escape through sleep. Kayla settled in next to me, responding through the night to help me find as much comfort as possible.

Chapter 10

Mayo Days: Wednesday

I Had To Get Up Sometime

November 5, 2008

Wednesday (by Kayla)

Mom had a really good night! She was able to get a lot of sleep after they switched her to a new pain medication. The new medication doesn't cause as much nausea as the previous stuff did either. The nurse woke her up every couple of hours to take her vitals and give more pain medicine, but she was able to quickly fall back asleep when the nurse left.

Her evening nurse was nice enough to show me where I could get ice chips, linens for the cot, and towels last night. That allowed us to be a little more self-sufficient and not as dependent on the nurses for the little things like that.

Today the doctors took her bandages off and the incision is healing well. We were also able to wash her face and arms with a wash cloth I found last night. Later today they are going to get her up into a chair.

For those of you wondering about her new hair-do ... there is a narrow strip about two inches wide or so that is shaved with an incision several inches long behind her ear. It is a much smaller bald patch than we were initially thinking.

4:30 PM - Mom sat up ... then stood up ... then sat in a chair next to the bed. She experienced minimal dizziness and was able to sit up for 10 minutes before moving back to the bed. The doctors and nurses are telling us patience is important and it will just take time.

Comments

So good to hear you had a good night; hope Kayla and your dad & brother did as well. You will feel so much better when you are able to sit up, just be good and don't try to "overachieve"—ha, like you could help it! :)

I'm so happy the operation went well and you are getting some rest. Hopefully, the nausea and dizziness will go away soon. Having Kayla, your brother and dad there must be such a comfort. You are still on my prayer list—as someone said in an earlier message—Jesus is the Great Healer! Amen!

The wound behind my right ear felt funny to me, numb to the touch, with a long line of twenty-nine staples. I tried to feel where my skin stopped and staples started. It was all pulled into a ridge of fortitude to ensure closure of my brain. The nurses gave me cute pink stocking caps to wear for protection of the wound as well as to cover my horrifically dirty hair. My normally free-flowing tresses clung to my head, still caked with surgery debris.

They had talked about getting me up sometime that day. I was terrified though, as I was getting sick so easily. They gave me Dramamine, but it wasn't enough. Reluctantly, I agreed to sit on the edge of the bed. Lifting my head from the pillow to sit made me dizzy. It took forever to get my legs over the side. Sitting made me weak. Once I relaxed a bit, it felt good to feel my legs dangle, free from the compression equipment that had bound them. It felt good to sit upright. I had accomplished as much as I thought I could for one day. I had made a huge step forward.

However, shortly after sitting up, Kayla asked me if I wanted to move to the chair. I said no way, but she pointed out that the chair was only one step away. She urged me to just stand and turn to sit. When she pointed out that if I sat in the chair they would change my sheets, I perked up a bit. There is little in the hospital as refreshing as clean sheets. I sat in the chair just long enough to have the sheets changed, and then I was back in bed. Kayla was an incredible motivator. I was exhausted. I wondered how I would ever be back in the woods, walking my dogs. How I would ever be mobile and pain free again?

Pain management was confusing. They kept changing the drugs and combinations to try to give me the maximum relief with the least amount of nausea. I was constantly confused about which drug was to kill pain and which were to kill peaks, or what they called breakthrough pain. I was pretty good at keeping up with time though, as I knew every four hours I could have narcotics, and every six hours I could have Tylenol. My family tracked everything, always ensuring nausea medication was included. I waited eagerly for each dose and then waited for relief, which seemed marginal and anticlimactic.

Lesson Learned
Never underestimate the power of caring.

Al went home on Wednesday when he was satisfied I was alive. My Dad and Kayla had routines established quickly. Kayla spent the night. Dad came in the morning to relieve her so she could return to the hotel for a shower and break. They would go to lunch together for some camaraderie. Dad would head to the cafeteria midafternoon for pie and to call Mom. He would stay with me in the evening so Kayla could call her husband before taking on the night shift. I was rarely alone in the room.

Even through my fog, I was keenly aware of how kind, attentive, and caring everyone was. The nurses were used to seeing such carnage and told me how well I was doing. Kayla always pushed me to do one more thing. My Dad was always there just to talk or to crack a joke. They saw me, and not the horrible, ragdoll me. All people involved with my care accepted the normalcy of handing me a barf pan or cleaning up what missed it.

That day I started to keep my Blackberry at my side and sent quick notes to some of my friends. It felt good to have a small link with the outside world. Getting surprised replies made me smile. Smile inside even though my face was half frozen.

Chapter 11

Mayo Days: Thursday

The Face in the Mirror

November 6, 2008

Thursday (by Kayla)

Mom slept well last night and the nurse allowed her to sleep for longer stretches at a time. The doctors seem to have found a pain medication combination that makes the pain bearable for her. She has also begun to eat soft foods, which is a step up from the clear diet.

She has four walks planned for today. We will start small and work our way up as she can tolerate it. She is looking forward to wearing the slippers she got for the hospital on her walks and impressed the nurses yesterday with them when she moved to the chair.

She is constantly reminding herself that this requires patience and time to heal.

12:00 PM - It is lunch time and Mom has sat in the chair next to the bed since breakfast. She has also walked to the door and back twice already—two more walks to go!

5:30 PM - Well...so much for being an over-achiever. Mom was done with 3 of her 4 planned walks for the day, and then her doctor came in, saw how well she was doing and added two more for the day. Now she just completed walk 4 of the 6 required. This afternoon they also sent a chocolate milkshake for her, which was probably one of the first good things coming out of the kitchen other than Jell-O!

Comments

Sally, your progress sounds EXCELLENT! Don't try too much ... but having solid food has you one step closer to chocolate! Keep up the good work! Kayla, I hope you're getting some rest!!

Hi Sally—Glad to hear you are moving about. It sounds like you are making great progress. Take it easy on the walks and don't get frustrated. Patience is a virtue. Take things a day at a time.

Hi Sally! Just wanted to remind you that it's been exactly 4 days since you had BRAIN SURGERY. You are making incredible progress, even though you may not feel like it.

Pain medication? Patience? Slippers? Going for walks? What do you think this is? A SPA vacation?!? ENOUGH lollygagging around. Yea, yea, yea.. it's less than a week, only 2.5 days since you got out of surgery ... waa, waa, waa ... but it's been over 64 hours, almost 4,000 minutes ... almost 250 TRILLION nanoseconds ... and counting!! It seems like you'd at least have time to post pictures of the slippers?! Seriously, you know what happens when you try to push the "project' too fast. The body and brain are amazing things, but take time and energy to heal.

Enjoy the present. And seriously, we must see those slippers. We're thinking about you.

On the wall of the hospital room was a white board. Every morning, the nurse or aide would come in and write the current day, date, and the names of my nurses. The board had a section for activities that I was to push myself for. On Thursday, I got up for four walks, while trying to build strength for my eyelid implantation procedure they said I might have that day.

Food tasted wrong, with a metallic bite caused by my nerves being confused. Soda tasted terrible. I loved Jell-O, as long as it wasn't green. The nutritionist brought me a milk shake. It was the first thing that actually tasted kind of good to me. After seeing me consume it, my family tracked down the nutritionist and asked that they bring me one with dinner every day.

I made it to a mirror for the first time. I knew it would be bad, and it was. The right side of my face sagged. The entire right side of my neck was swollen with no contours from the top of my head to my shoulder. I looked 80 years old. I remembered the smile I used to have. I didn't even try to smile so the face in the mirror looked back without emotion or motion. I looked into my sad, blank eyes. I looked like I felt. *Oh well. It's as bad as I imagined.* I looked away. What was God thinking?

On Thursday, I became frustrated with my bladder. They removed my catheter. I knew from past hospital stays I needed to have my bladder and bowels moving before I could leave. We learned through the day that, my bladder had "gone to sleep" due to the day-long anesthesia for surgery. It didn't want to start working. That day I learned that Mayo Clinic has a department staffed with people whose sole job is to drain bladders. When I was unable to go, they came in twice a day, or as needed, to empty me out. It was embarrassing, but a definite relief.

I waited all afternoon to be called for my eyelid procedure. I was trying to rest up to have the strength. At the end of the day, they came in and said due to an emergency, they couldn't fit me in. It would probably be Monday before they could do it. I was disappointed, but relieved I would be able to regain more strength before the procedure.

After Al returned home, he called regularly to check on me. I knew I'd missed his call one time on Thursday when I was alone in the room, unable to reach the ringing phone. I called him from my Blackberry, which I always kept within reach. When he answered, I said "What's happening?" which was our standard way of greeting each other. I have to say he was actually giddy about how I sounded. He was excited and said he could tell I was okay and I was improving. I heard relief in his voice and thought to myself that if he heard improvement, there must really be improvement. Later he told me he really knew for the first time I was still me inside and was going to be okay at that moment on the phone. My brother doesn't get giddy.

Chapter 12

Mayo Days: Friday

Overwhelmed

November 7, 2008

Friday (by Kayla)

We woke up to a winter wonderland this morning. It was a good night and we both slept well. The nurse last night told us how we could get on demand movies, so we checked those out before bed ... or at least part of a movie as neither of us could stay awake for it.

Today the goal is movement and lots of it.

On Friday morning, when Dr. Link came in, Kayla told him we were hoping for a shower today. She mentioned that I was a bit reluctant. I said to the doctor, "I kind of like my filth."

He smiled, "Well, you'll understand if we talk to you from the doorway from now on." I liked him. He had a sense of humor and seemed to get my humor. I felt comforted in his calm presence.

Late that morning, at Kayla's continued urging, I had my first seated shower. She said I was starting to smell bad, my hair still caked with post-surgical debris. A nurse came in to help me. It turned out no regular-sized shower chairs were available. So into the room they wheeled an oversized chair. The chair was plastic, on wheels, with a hole in the seat. Well, I pictured myself in the chair and chuckled.

I shuffled into the bathroom. The nurse helped me undress and sit in the huge chair. I was cold, so I huddled. I was afraid I might fall through the hole in the chair, so I didn't move while seated. The nurse turned on the water and gently washed my head. I had a lot of blood and stuff caked at the back of my head. She got some of it out, but there was much more left for the next time. She washed my back, and gave me a washcloth and the showerhead for my front. I remember thinking I must look pretty pathetic all huddled under the trickling water. It felt incredibly good. I felt clean for the first time since surgery.

Kayla was relieved that I smelled better. She knew a shower would feel good to me and help to lift my spirits, if only a little bit. I was exhausted but clean. My family left for lunch to let me rest.

I had barely gotten settled back in bed, spent for the day, when a nurse came in and told me I was supposed to be in the procedure room in a half hour for the eyelid procedure. What?

I was barely able to get out of bed, and was having a lot of problems with nausea. I agreed to the shower because I didn't think they would be doing my eyelid that day. I was terrified at the thought of having my eyelid slit open for any reason. Although I wanted to get it done well before being released from the hospital, as I couldn't imagine having the stamina to come back in anytime soon for a procedure. Prior to surgery, it had been predicted I would go home on Friday, and here I was immobile, unable to pee, and headed for a procedure.

The nurse whisked me to the procedure area in a wheelchair, my eyes closed. I clung to my barf pan, which I had been using several times a day. It was my security for dizziness and its aftermath. She wheeled me into a small waiting room and left me. There were two other patients, who looked pretty rough from whatever they had experienced to date in the hospital. It struck me that, as bad as they looked, I looked worse. I didn't look like a vibrant woman of fifty-one. I was a haggard woman with a half-paralyzed face, stocking cap on my head, and IV bruises on my hands.

The Eyelid Procedure

I was wheeled into the procedure room and cautiously rose from my wheelchair and sat in a reclining procedure chair. A young, energetic female resident started the procedure. A couple minutes into it, the doctor arrived. They chatted. He was giving her pointers on the procedure. At one point, he remarked, "We don't usually do this with patients who are awake!" What? I was baffled. I guess they assumed since I was full of drugs and still had anesthesia in my system from nine-hour brain surgery, local anesthesia would be sufficient. I had to agree that going under general anesthesia was not a good idea for me at that point. I encouraged them to continue.

Despite trying to power through, twice I had to stop them for more local anesthetic. Each shot in my eyelid made me squeamish. The doctor remarked, "You are doing great. They make 'em tough in Michigan." I groaned in response. They were kind and gentle.

I was wishing it to be finished. It felt we must be approaching the length of time they said it would take when the resident said, "You are doing great. We are now half way done. I just have to close up now." I sighed with resignation. Only halfway there? Oh, my. I continued my attempts at relaxation and steady breathing. I tried to tap into my Lamaze training from pregnancy over twenty years ago. Relax, breathe. Unclench my fists into relaxed hands.

Finally, it was done. I slowly moved back to the wheelchair and she opened the door to wheel me out of the room. Standing there was my male nurse for the day, Don. He was leaning on a desk. I remarked, "Did I keep you waiting?" He had come down to the procedure area looking for me when I hadn't returned to my room as expected. The procedure had taken longer than planned. He was competent, attentive, and caring. He stepped up, and pushed my wheelchair back up to my room. I chuckled when it struck me like he was waiting, somewhere impatiently, as if I were at a spa treatment instead of a surgical procedure. It was great to have someone who laughed with me. Once again, I felt cared for by the nurses and staff.

It seemed nurses were constantly in my face with pills to swallow. I was lying in bed, struggling to drink from my flat and motionless position. Pills kept getting caught on my tongue. Drinking always ended up being a bath. And sitting made my head hurt. As I lay, heavily drugged, struggling with my facial muscles, I persevered and managed to drink using a straw.

By day four, I was confident my straw management was under control. However, all morning it was a major struggle every time I tried to use a straw. The nurses were encouraging and patient, "No rush," etc., assuming the problem was me. Finally, I said, "Bring me a new straw, maybe this one has a hole." They "humored" me and brought a new straw. No problem! It worked great. So all morning I had been frustrated, thinking I was going backwards ... and it wasn't really my fault because there WAS a hole in the straw!

For another night I settled into my hospital bed. I wore my eye bubble to ensure my eye remained moist. My eye was swollen, the weight providing relief but feeling strange. I slept a little more between nurse visits with pain medication. I hadn't made it out of the hospital by Friday, which was the early projection. I wasn't beating expectations for a rapid recovery. I didn't really care.

Chapter 13

Mayo Days: The Weekend

Quiet Healing

November 8, 2008

Saturday (by Kayla)

Another good night. There was talk today that Mom may be released tomorrow or Monday—it all depends on which doctor we talk to. There is no lack of doctors who are taking an interest in her case; after all it is a teaching institution.

Mom is struggling with patience. She is also discouraged at how hard it is to just do simple things when you are trying to recover from brain surgery.

Happy Saturday from Sally. Today was a slow "doctor day" because we only saw five doctors ... must be a weekend. Mom took a long nap after lunch that seems to have re-energized her. Tonight the plan is to go to a movie, get frozen cokes and popcorn—okay so maybe it will just be on demand movies with orange sherbet, but we will have fun!

I am still staying with her every night and Grandpa comes over all day. I am able to get away for a couple of breaks while he is here and we go out for lunch together after Mom gets her lunch. Al went home to check on Grandma, who is watching Gina, Paulo, and Gabby.

In all the excitement, I realized today that I failed to mention Mom had a shower yesterday. She said it felt really good, but was exhausting. Today we counted her staples, 29 in total to close the 5-6 inch incision behind her ear.

November 9, 2008
Sunday (by Kayla)

Mom is resting well and every night the nurses let her sleep longer. She is beginning to take fewer narcotics and transitioning some to other types of pain medicine. This morning the nurse helped her with another shower, which felt wonderful.

Grandpa and I are sleeping well, but both suffering from a bit of a head cold we have picked up somewhere. I am sure it is a result of the quick transition in weather and the dry winter air that has settled in here. I found the laundry facilities today at the hotel—free washers, free dryers, and free detergent—a pleasant surprise.

Comments

Patience is hard to come by. But you know, Sally, that if you were to be giving advice to anyone else in your shoes you KNOW it's what you have to have! I'm praying for patience, recovery, chocolate ice cream and chocolate milk shakes. It's amazing to me that it's been less than a week and already talk about going home! Keep up the good work!

29 Staples and no "Easy Button"!!! Imagine that! Take your time & eat lots of ice cream (everyone should eat ice cream at least once a day!) Enjoy your movies!

Hi! I just walked the dogs, I couldn't comment until I took them out today. I thought of you Sally, using every ounce of strength to heal and Kayla there at your side and how you'd both rather be out walking. Well, maybe not in this crazy weather, but I honor your efforts and whatever you'd rather be doing! Keep up the fight. It felt great to walk them and they didn't seem to mind the cold or wet that quickly got their little jacket things wet. I also got wet as I once again got tangled at one point and stepped into a rather deep puddle which splashed the rest of my leg. It's so fun to see people's expressions as they drive by and stare at those cute little dogs and probably wonder what the heck I am doing with 3 dogs, since I brought Chester along too. Gina was the leader today and Paulo was happy to let her. Maybe it's that low body fat that kept her wanting to move quickly to stay warm! Safe and comfortable travels to you all whenever your plethora of docs releases you. Sounds like you have a good progression through pain meds and sleeping, showering and exercising. It's baby steps, but you are moving! Great job. God Bless your healing and your healers.

The weekend had a different feel to it at the hospital. The doctors were different, and less familiar with each case on their floors. They'd stop in each morning and night, unaware of any release plans.

I walked around the hallway several times each day. At first I needed two people to help steady me. Eventually, I was able to walk with the help of just Kayla or my father. I saw a little sign with a snowflake hanging on my room door. A nurse explained it was there to signify that I was at risk for falling. I sure didn't want to fall, so I really clung to whoever was helping me walk.

Kayla kept prompting me to try to pee. That was obviously the one thing keeping me in the hospital. I would try, but then get tired of sitting up. Once after a few minutes of sitting on the toilet, she asked why I was ready to quit. I said "I'm bored." Instead of helping me back to my bed, she came into the bathroom with a chair and sat in front of me, asking, "So, if you're bored, I'm here to entertain. Do you want to play cards?" She kept me company, but I still wasn't able to go. We laughed about her willingness to do ANYTHING to help me recover.

Lesson Learned

Learn patience—you will improve. Don't try to rush things.

Kayla and I tried to watch movies. However, I was taking drugs and couldn't keep my eyes open. I had no idea what movie we were watching, but it looked psychedelic through the narcotics and eye bubble's condensation. Kayla was exhausted herself and gave up pretty early. She turned the TV off and went to bed.

She stayed with me Friday and Saturday nights. However, her health was going downhill. She was getting worn down from nights with constantly interrupted sleep and got the sniffles from laying on her cot right by the window. Everything was catching up with her. On Sunday night I urged her to stay in her hotel room. We were hoping to go home Monday, and I wanted her to get rest. That evening, she reluctantly left for her hotel. She almost turned around three times but kept going. She kept reminding herself of the advice that unless you took care of yourself you wouldn't be able to take care of your loved one in the hospital.

During the night, in my confusion, I wondered why the nurse hadn't come yet. It took several minutes and nod-offs before remembering

I hadn't yet pushed the nurse call button. I had gotten used to just squeaking to get Kayla's attention, who then called the nurse.

I couldn't have asked for better caregivers than my daughter and father. I was grateful beneath my pain, confusion, and disillusionment.

Chapter 14

Mayo Days: Monday

Heading Home

November 10, 2008
Monday (by Kayla)
We are hopefully heading back towards Michigan today. We will also have to see how Mom does in the car and what time she is released—both factors in how far we make it toward home today.

We are all ready to be home!

The anesthesiologist and others had told me the hospitalization would be a few days. For me it was a full week. I could tell my family wanted to leave. I felt like such a burden to them. When it reached a full week on Monday, I decided it was time to go home. I had seen the disappointment on my family's faces whenever another day was added.

The doctor came in that morning, still concerned because my bladder hadn't woken up. He talked to me about the alternatives. They could put the catheter back in. The second option was to learn "self-catheterization." Or they could keep me in the hospital longer. I looked him in the eye, and said, "Nothing personal, you guys have been great, but I want to go home."

He seemed surprised at my determination to go home. I told him I had watched the instructional video on TV twice, and had received training from the urology department. He said okay, and headed out to complete my paperwork. I didn't want to stay any longer and, despite being squeamish about what I would have to do, I had learned how to care for myself.

I was continuing to navigate a tricky balance. I was supposed to push myself, but when I did I was sick to my stomach. Whenever I would say "I don't feel good," my family took it as a trigger to get a pan under my mouth, immediately. I didn't feel nauseous, but when I got that feeling, vomiting wasn't far behind. Evidently my body was so confused that I had a new feeling for sickness. Over the days, I got sick less and less.

On Monday, as we waited for my discharge approval, my father and I were alone in my room. I had been up and around a lot, and then knew I needed to sit for a while. That new nauseous feeling came over me, and I said "I don't feel good. I think I am going to get sick." With all the activity that morning, my trusty barf pans were misplaced. We both scanned the room quickly. Finally, both of our eyes settled on a large waste basket. Dad grabbed it, reaching me with it just in time. Well, it was effective as a container and solved our immediate problem! As I was getting sick, a nurse came into my room. She looked at the large waste basket, me purging into it, and looked concerned. I looked at the huge waste basket in my hands, and started laughing.

I think she put a stop on my discharge for a couple hours to ensure that I felt better. We were left alone for what seemed like hours. Right after lunch, the word came that I could leave. Kayla helped me get dressed in my sharp new sweat pants and jacket we had purchased the month before, and out we went. My father had filled my prescriptions and was waiting with the car.

As Kayla wheeled me down the elevator and through the lobby, I looked at the people as we passed. They all looked normal. Many averted their eyes when they saw me. "I'm guessing they're all thankful to not be me right now." I knew I looked bad, really bad. I had a swollen neck and face that was immobile. My eye was still swollen and now blackening from the weight implantation. My arms lay loosely on my thighs, and I held my head gingerly between tense yet slumped shoulders. Only my eyes moved as we rolled through toward freedom.

At the main door of the hospital, there was an orderly who assisted me out of my wheelchair and into the back seat of the car. I said, "For some reason, my family won't let me drive."

I guess he didn't get the joke. "Did you have heart surgery?"

"No, brain surgery."

"Oh."

Take Me Home!

The doctors had said when I was released, I should stay in the area for one night. That made sense when I thought I would be released over the weekend, but by Monday we were ready to go home. I told them when I was released, I wanted them to put me in the car and drive toward Michigan. I knew if I only crossed the street to a hotel I would worry all night about the car ride the next day.

Finally, it was 2:00 PM and we were on the road for our nine-hour drive. I sat in the back, eyes closed. I didn't dare open them. I had no idea how my body would be reacting to the car ride. I braced for feeling sick, but found I was okay. After about two hours, we pulled over so Kayla could give me more pain medication with diced pears so my stomach wouldn't be empty. As we took off, I slowly opened my eyes and started to look around. I wasn't sick! "Kayla, look! My eyes are open and I'm not sick!'

"You are being very brave, Mom."

"Yea, I'm getting cocky."

As we continued on, I was doing okay. What a relief. After dark, we stopped at a Wendy's for dinner. I didn't want to go in for many reasons including my slowness and my appearance. Since my bladder wasn't working anyway, and I didn't feel like I had to go, I stayed at the car. With Kayla's help I got out and walked to the rear of the car and back. That was enough. They got me a baked potato. It tasted great after a week of hospital food. Once Kayla and Dad were filled with food, we headed out again.

When we got to Chicago, it was nighttime. The lights of the oncoming cars started to bother me, even through closed eyes. I mentioned it to Kayla and she told me to pull my hood down over my eyes. That fixed things, and I was ready for the rest of the trip. I was proud of my daughter, who always came up with simple solutions for what to me seemed like complex problems in my narcotic stupor.

The trip took about nine hours. My father drove all the way. Kayla kept checking on me and giving me pain medication and diced pears periodically. Everyone was exhausted, but delighted when we drove in my driveway. I was surprised to see Al had driven to my house to help them get me into the house. In addition, Kayla's husband, Mark, was there to pick her up. It was a great homecoming.

I was worried about my mom, because I didn't think she really understood how bad I was. I could barely walk, and my face looked frightening with its right side sagging. When the car stopped I moved faster than I had for a week to get out. My mother looked delighted as she rushed into the garage, and then instantly froze and teared up when she saw me emerge from the car with a hood pulled over greasy hair, frozen and swollen face and neck, with awkward movements.

"Oh dear. You look so miserable," and she hugged me.

I leaned onto her and we hugged. We both wept for a minute, my first tears since surgery.

I looked like death warmed over, but Al thought I was quite improved since he last saw me a few days before in the hospital. Mark was in the background, delighted to see his wife. He had been prepared by Kayla for seeing me, but he was clearly shocked. I looked bad. There was no denying it. Seeing myself in their unaccustomed eyes told me what I already knew. I saw each person control their reaction as I stepped through the doors. I was alert inside my still face.

Mom asked me where I wanted to lie down. They were prepared to settle me in on a couch if I wasn't up to going upstairs. However, I was determined to be in my bed that night. So I started up the stairs. Al was behind me and remarked at how well I was doing by myself. I was tiring fast. When I was about three steps from the top, I said to him, "Could you give me a little push for the rest of the stairs?"

He laughed, "Really?"

"Yes, I'm running out of steam."

He then gently pushed me from behind as I climbed those last steps. Once at the top of the stairs, I stepped into my bedroom and sat on the bench at the end of my bed. I was home.

Gina jumped up on my lap instantly. She shook. I petted her and caught my breath. My family all came into the bedroom and we talked for a few minutes about the trip.

Kayla was still my primary caregiver, and was protective of me. She was eager to get home with Mark, so she explained things to my mother to turn my care over to her. She helped me into the bathroom for my self-catheterization. I argued because I was so tired, but she convinced me as we were already beyond the recommended time for draining. Somehow I found the strength to attend to my private duties. I then, with help, crawled into bed.

I can't describe how good my bed felt. I was exhausted, and still taking pain medication every four hours. Everyone left except for my parents who were planning to live with me as long as I needed help. I was once again overwhelmed by the love of my family. I wondered how anyone else got through surgery without such support. It was hard to see Kayla leave—I felt so bonded to her. But it was time for her to get back to her life, and to recover from an oncoming cold. She planned to come back over the weekend to stay with me and give my parents a break.

My father went straight to bed. He was exhausted from the drive and needed his sleep. I know he was relieved to have completed that long drive, especially at age seventy-four. My mother got things settled for me. She put the dogs downstairs. I love my dogs, but I agreed I was in no condition to share my bed with them yet. I needed my sleep to be as uninterrupted as possible. Paulo whimpered for a few minutes, but he settled down and went to sleep.

I returned to my rag doll position in the bed. I had extra pillows to help relieve the pain on my left side. I couldn't lean too far to the right though or my head would hurt where they had drilled a week ago. My mother helped me arrange all the pillows. She set up a TV tray by my bed and lined up my medications and water. Once settled, I sent her to bed. I assured her I could call if I needed anything.

Seeing her in action took me back to my childhood. Whenever my brother or I were home sick from school, Mom would make a big production of it. She would put sheets on the couch so we could lay downstairs. She would get a TV tray set up next to us. She would scurry back and forth between the kitchen and our special bed bringing soda, soup, or whatever we wanted. She would regularly shake the mercury down in the thermometer and take temperatures. She was a great nurse. Once again, at fifty-one, I was receiving Mom's diligence and attention to detail.

I lay in bed for a few minutes awake, looking at the ceiling. I was overwhelmed with pain, but I felt appreciation for my home. Laying there felt incredibly good. My bed, my pillow, and my house. I looked at the ceiling and remembered looking at it over a week ago wondering what I would be going through at Mayo. Surgery was now behind me. The tumor was removed. I had had no idea how hard this was going to be. I had had no idea when I last looked at that ceiling what it would really be like.

I slept for a few hours. I awoke abruptly in the night, unable to lift my head from the pillow because it hurt so badly. I called out, and my father heard me and came in. He gave me a pain pill. We wrote down the time of my medication in a little notebook. After waiting a few minutes for the pain to subside just a bit, with his help, I shuffled to the bathroom. I was able to urinate without catheterization. Just being home seemed to let my body relax enough to just start the return to normal. After all my training and angst, I had only had to do self-catheterization once.

Eventually, Morning Arrived

I had woken every few hours, but sleep was good. I had strange dreams, in which I was normal. Then I would awaken in pain. The dogs slipped upstairs as soon as the gate was opened at the bottom of the stairs when my parents got up. They seemed to sense something was wrong. They jumped on my bed and both immediately lay down. They instinctively knew I needed them to be gentle. They slept without moving for hours.

In the afternoon, my friend Margie came by to walk my dogs. I heard my father invite her upstairs to say Hi to me. I was terrified. Just as they were coming up the stairs, I got sick again. I was barfing into my ever-ready barf pan. Between hurls, I said, "I'm getting sick," but my father couldn't hear me until he came into the room to tell me Margie was coming in.

Calm as a cucumber, Dad said, "Oh, she's getting sick. Just give us a minute, Margie, and we'll get her cleaned up." He was used to my sickness patterns at that time. He took my pan, gave me a washcloth, and I quickly cleaned up. With that, he told her to come in.

Terror. I mean core terror filled me. Here I was, sick and terrible looking. Margie was the first non-family member to see me with half my face paralyzed. I had hoped it would be temporary and start to improve before I saw anyone. But here she was. I'll never forget her standing by my bed. She told me it was going to be okay. She put her hand on my blankets over my knee. She pointed out it was early, and I needed to give it time.

She left, and I felt relief. I had seen my friend and she accepted me, even in my new form. She had reassured me. What I didn't know until later is she was freaked out by the fear she saw in my eyes. She knew her neighbor had had the same type of tumor and called her as soon as she got home.

Her neighbor acknowledged it was a tough journey and the surgery had really knocked her down. But over time there was hope. She had fully recovered, and regained her facial movement. It helped Margie, who sent me an e-mail to reassure me that things would look up for me.

Trips to the bathroom were still the extent of my exhausting day. I didn't have the focus or vision for reading so I watched some TV and napped. Evening brought hope of a reasonable night's sleep and a better next day. Night was welcome as it did bring much-needed rest for my brain, body, and morale.

Chapter 15

Hello, World

I slept better that night. We had established a pattern. I would sleep for about four hours. Either Mom or Dad would come in when I turned on my light or called. They would give me oxycodone and after a few minutes I would raise my head from my pillow and go to the bathroom. It really was that painful. I could not lift my head from the pillow without a dose of narcotics.

I was still unbalanced. I worried about getting across the room alone without falling. My mother found a ski pole in the basement, and I used it as a cane to steady myself across the room. I felt much more independent to just go to the bathroom alone. Such a simple thing, but a huge step for me. It seemed every time I went to the bathroom during the night I would drop the ski pole noisily on the bathroom's tile floor.

"Sally, you okay?"

"I'm fine. Sorry."

Thursday was the first day I wanted to use my computer. So I had my mother bring me my laptop in bed. It took a long time to type anything, one key at a time, but it felt good. My hand shook and I didn't have control of it for typing. I entered my first blog entry. Somehow it just popped into my head that this first entry after surgery was like the first time I learned programming. A lot of effort for a little result. But its significance couldn't be denied.

November 13, 2008

Hello World

For you programmers out there, you will remember how exciting it was the first time you got a computer to say "Hello World" through programming.

That is how I feel right now getting online for the first time since brain surgery.

First, thanks. I hope you recognize how many feelings are in that word.

Second, typing this has taken a long time. I now appreciate you "hunt and peckers." My fine motor skills are at a low point that will take a long time to reskill.

Third, I am learning patience.

More later. Love, Sally

Comments

Well done my friend.

Kayla said ... Back online ... going downstairs ... taking showers alone ... wow! Will I even recognize you tonight when Mark and I get there?

So glad to hear the long ride back was uneventful and traffic free. Thanks so much for setting up this blog Sally, and Kayla for keeping it up. There's no place like home, there's no place like home, and there's no place like home! Welcome back.

I am glad to hear that your experience with bright lights, cold steel and folks with sharp knifes cutting on your noggin delivered an outstanding outcome. I had little doubt given your tenacity that you would not bounce back from this one in short order. I will always remember the story you told me of getting tossed from the horse at a gallop, foot getting caught in the stirrup and being dragged a crossed some ditch and saying "I really need to get that left hoof re-shoed at some point." One tough lady I told myself. Great to see you are now at home and on the road to Wellville.

Margie called another friend of ours, Nancy. She told Nancy I needed their support. So that evening, Nancy came by with dinner for me and my parents. She brought me a cane that their family wasn't using. She offered a walker, but I told her literally using a walker was yesterday. I had improved enough in one day to feel confident with a cane.

She came upstairs to visit while her husband Steve walked my dogs. From upstairs, I heard Steve express good humored distaste when he saw Gina wearing a University of Michigan sweatshirt despite his loyalty to Michigan State. We all laughed, and Steve went ahead and walked Gina, hoping he wasn't seen. In twenty-four hours, my attitude had changed from fright to pleasure when my friend Nancy came in the room.

"You look great! I don't know what Margie was talking about." She had also accepted me, despite how screwed up I felt and looked. Having the support of my friends was amazing and a huge help in starting to accept myself. Maybe I could go in public again sometime in the future.

Lesson Learned

Friends do want to help. Accept help from anyone who offers. Think of things they can do, like walk the dogs.

My mother marveled at how I was already up and down the stairs. Never without calling my folks to watch my descent or ascent. It did feel good to see some improvement. I was getting mobile.

Late in the week, I needed to call AT&T about my phone, TV, and Internet service. I was on the phone for about an hour and a half. I still couldn't write. When the AT&T person on the phone told me something I had to write, I tried but couldn't read my own writing. I called my mother in, and dictated to her what they told me so she could write it for me. As soon as I was done, I took a long nap. I was totally exhausted and in pain.

On Friday, I struggled with authenticity. We had told the world my surgery was successful. However, I felt we had sugarcoated how poorly I was really doing. Kayla and I had agreed she would put all positive information in her posts and leave anything negative for me to post when I was ready. I was ready.

November 14, 2008

Happy Friday

Doing okay today. I am learning patience. I can safely say I have never done anything this hard. I can now explain what it must feel like to have been run over by a bus—twice!!

Today, though, I can say I feel good. Really.

Regarding my prognosis: I will return to Mayo in three months to evaluate my progress.

Damage: Right facial weakness, Good news is that the nerve is intact. Part of the weakness is from brain swelling and part is from nerve damage which will improve over time. What we do not know is how long or how much will return. Facial weakness means the right side of my face doesn't work right: eye doesn't close and my mouth doesn't work right. Think of all the money I will save on BOTOX in the future with no wrinkles!!

Damage: Right arm weakness, Good news is it will strengthen with time. This weakness is because they had to move part of my brain (Cerebellum) aside to get to the tumor.

Damage: Right hearing gone, no good news here. My left ear will only choose to hear what I want to hear so you'll have make it worth hearing (grin)!!

Damage: The Brain Tumor has been eradicated. No good news for the tumor, which now lives in a research lab in Mayo and was confirmed to be benign. They got it OUT of my head. That is only great news to all.

So you will notice the theme here is time. LOTS of it. Along with the life lesson of patience.

Sally

The weekend came and Kayla and Mark came to stay with me. It was good to have them spend time with me. Margie had brought a casserole on Friday. Kayla and Mark came upstairs to eat dinner with me, since I wasn't going downstairs much yet. It tasted great, and I enjoyed their company. I sincerely appreciated their acceptance and effort that they took to make me feel comfortable. I was still having some difficulty eating, and constantly used napkins to clean my mouth.

Just as I was feeling more content, I had that bad feeling in my stomach. I said, "I don't feel good." I went into the bathroom and just sat on a stool by the sink. Kayla, always the practical one, grabbed my barf pan and gave it to me just in time. I lost everything I had eaten. I was embarrassed, and I know it was difficult for Kayla and Mark, but they never let on. They just said it was no problem. Kayla helped get me cleaned up and back in bed.

On Sunday, my brother and his family came to check on me. It was clear Al had not prepared his wife, Lovedia, for my facial paralysis. She did her best to control her expression, but was clearly startled by my appearance. She stammered, "It must be good to be home!"

Frederick, my nephew, walked in, gave me a good look and said, "Aunt Sally, you still look like you." With that, he grabbed the remote control and started surfing TV channels for his favorite shows.

The rest of the weekend was a bit less eventful. I still couldn't write, so I had Kayla fill out my checks for me to pay some bills. I slowly went downstairs to the main floor at least once a day. I was focused on healing and took long naps. My eye weight was doing its job but I still needed a lot of drops and closed eye time.

Each day brought more relief and healing. I started to cut down on and then eliminate narcotics from my daily routine. My stomach was still incredibly touchy, and I hoped getting off narcotics would help. I took nonstop Dramamine, Tylenol, and Motrin, but I was able to limit my narcotic usage to a couple times a week.

On Tuesday, at two weeks, was my first venture out of the house. I had to get the staples removed from my head, so I went to see my general physician. It was a huge step for me to actually go somewhere. My face looked quite saggy, and I needed a cane to walk. However, after my folks had driven me to the doctor's office, I was able to walk into my appointment. The staple removal was easy. My doctor referred me to physical therapy for my face.

I went to the physical therapy office and got started right away. The therapist massaged my face, and then showed me exercises to do. It seemed quite futile to do exercises where my fingers actually did the work of moving my face. She ordered an electrical stimulator, which I used for about a month to shock the muscles of my face. There were theories it would help. I would find out later that what I was doing was the worst possible thing to do for facial nerve healing.

November 21, 2008

SLOW is the word of the day

It is like the brain surgery drained the energy out of me. At the end of the day I am exhausted. Then I reflect on the day and recollect going down the stairs was the biggest event. I can't explain it. I did make it to the end of my driveway on Wednesday!!

I am doing better every day. But better is relative to how far I fell off the cliff. . . .

Late, but consistent with my theme of slow, and due to popular demand, here's a picture of the slippers.

Pretty styling, not to mention the pj's.

WARNING—not for the squeamish.

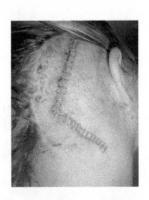

This is before the staples were removed. They were taken out on Tuesday. It did not hurt because Mayo sent a special removal tool with me for my doctor.

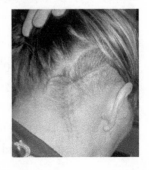

As you can see, it is already growing back and we'll probably only see the bottom part of the scar over time.

On Sunday, I was getting pretty self-sufficient with my showers. Kayla helped me get everything into the bathroom I needed. I started the shower, and carefully stepped in after she left the room. I was enjoying the shower, when I was suddenly overcome with emotion. I was so discouraged with the outcome of my surgery. I was overwhelmed with the constant pain. I was distraught about my face being half-paralyzed. I started to cry. I sobbed. I couldn't stop. I was trying to be careful because crying hurt my head. The narcotics were finally leaving my system and allowing me to feel emotion. Two weeks of no emotion were coming to an end.

I got out of the shower and slowly dressed myself. Kayla came upstairs and saw me crying. "Oh no, what's wrong?" I said I was just feeling emotional. I didn't know why. She said she had wondered why I hadn't cried before. She told me it was okay, that it was normal to cry after what I had been through.

Lesson Learned

A good attitude is important, but allowing grief for the old you is a better alternative than stuffing feelings down where they will eventually come out.

Another day, I cried when eating dinner with my parents. I started to accept I would have emotional outbursts, and accepted it as a normal part of healing. I would cry for a minute, and then be fine.

I loved having my parents live with me, but I felt driven to become independent. After a couple weeks of staying with me, I told them I thought I would be okay alone. They agreed that they were a phone call away, and they would come by every day to help me with anything necessary. They brought in the mail as I was unable to walk down the driveway yet. Mom did my laundry and Dad carried baskets up or down the stairs. We would watch the news for a while and visit. Dad would play with the dogs and cat while Mom tidied my kitchen. They were my link to the outside world and drove me to appointments.

November 24, 2008

One small step for mankind, one LARGE step for me

Three weeks out from surgery. I keep reminding myself of how far I've progressed. That helps me find patience and energy for how far I have yet to climb.

I am now living independently. I can't say enough about my family. I appreciate them so much. However, they have been so helpful that I'm now able to live alone again. That is, with their daily visits and steady phone calls.

As for the blog, I have been overwhelmed. I created it so that Kayla could update many people spread out through the world. However, I never expected the response from everyone. I couldn't even move in my hospital bed, but I had Kayla reading every one's comments from day one. I can't tell you how meaningful it was for me to know so many people cared. It really kept me going and feeling less isolated. Though there were times when you were all encouraging with my progress and I was thinking "You have no idea!!" (I think that's the overachiever in me.)

Okay, a bit sappy today. But necessary. I feel I have made a giant step by reaching this milestone of independence, and I had to say thanks—hoping you are still watching this blog!!

I was getting stronger every day. I was starting to gain control of my right hand. I could type a little faster. Definitely slower than in the past, but I was making fewer mistakes. I didn't understand the unrelenting pain. I wondered what was normal and where I would fit on the recovery scale.

Every day or so, I wrote out my alphabet. At first I had to concentrate hard and hold my hand as steady as possible. The letters were hard to recognize, but over a few weeks' time, my hand became better controlled and the letters became legible. I felt relieved when my handwriting improved to the point of being legible. It was still messy, but legible. Below is an image of my writing postsurgery and again after a year. My hand would improve over time but remain jumpy and a bit erratic.

Chapter 16

Things to Be
Thankful For

I was struggling with my faith at this point. I had thanked everyone in my blog, but was still lacking words for God. I certainly believed in Him, but why hadn't He intervened on my behalf? Why wasn't I able to skate right through brain surgery and continue my busy life? I was disappointed there was never a huge God moment during this experience. The closest was recognition that real life frequently doesn't have big moments, but many little moments that create a lifetime.

I spent quite a bit of time pondering my many questions and God's plan for my life. No, I couldn't see the future. However, I could see the past and how He had always provided for me. I had seen His hand working in my life for fifty years, and that track record gave me the faith I needed to once again put my life in His hands. I knew whenever I had become impatient waiting for guidance I almost always made the wrong decision. What I realized was summarized on my blog. God's plan would be revealed in time. His time. There was a plan though, I was confident of that.

November 25, 2008

Top Ten Things I Am Thankful For

10. Chocolate - this HAS to be on the list. Its only number 10 because I'm not up to my usual consumption. I am regaining my ability to eat and food is starting to taste good again. (Maybe this thanks should be for a lack of nausea, which seems to have finally gone.)

9. Physical Therapy - helpful? Who knows? But it feels like I'm DOING something.

8. Pets - My dogs, Gina and Paulo, Italian Greyhounds who think they are cats. And Kendra's cat Gabby, who thinks she is an Italian Greyhound. Figure that one out. Talk about companionship. They are happy to lay around with me all the time.

7. The incredible response to this blog—you have really blown me away with your comments and e-mails. This definitely has made this less lonely.

6. God's many answers to prayer - we can ask why the tumor, but given its existence, prayer has lifted me and provided for my family. I am amazed at their perseverance, which encourages me, and I know God has strengthened them. And I know things could have turned out much worse. (Look at how much I can type already!!)

5. The many people offering those prayers - thank you, thank you, thank you. Whether the simple or complex version, thank you. Again you have all blown me away.

4. People who choose Health Care as their career, such as Brain Surgery. Just think—it took these two guys and their team 9 hours to remove my tumor. Amazing patience and precision. I would have had it out in 10 minutes and left the poor patient reeling with problems!!

3. My family and my friends - who have been incredibly supportive. (And who have provided great food!!)

2. God's Plan for my life - Clarity normally comes after adversity, rarely in the midst of it. I am still very much in the middle now and look forward to someday looking back to see a purpose. I know it is there.

1. Faith - without it I wouldn't have the track record that has shown me in the past there clearly is a plan. Sometimes Faith steps in when feelings fail. I can't and won't pontificate grandly on why this happened to me and currently admit a preference to self-pity over a bigger grander purpose, but I do know God is here.

I am grateful for much in my life, but this list should give you an idea of what I'll be thankful for this Thanksgiving.

HAPPY THANKSGIVING!!

Sally

Comments

Kendra said ... oh mom, I love reading your blog. This is cool to see and it inspired me to do something similar. We'll see ... oh and nice use of "pontificate". Seriously, that's impressive for anyone, especially a recent brain surgery patient. Pontificate. Only my mother . . .

Sally I hope this finds you continuing to recover well and looking to the future. We said a prayer for you before dinner yesterday. Hope to see you soon.

I felt incredibly grateful for the support from everyone. I learned through e-mail and phone calls quite a few people were still following my blog. So I kept it up, trying to express my gratitude.

On Thanksgiving, I went to my parents' house for dinner. It was the first time I drove my car. I was probably the slowest and most cautious driver on the road that day. I had two miles to go in the country, so there was little risk of meeting traffic. It was snowy though, so I really took my time. Turning to the right and left at corners was slow. But I did it. The car felt so foreign. Had it ever been just easy to hop in the car and drive somewhere? It was clear I would have my father drive me to appointments for the near future.

Just as we sat down for dinner, I once again was overtaken by emotion. It was exacerbated by the new feeling of only having one eye tighten and tear. I got up, grabbed a tissue, and sat back down when under control. I honestly can't tell you I was either sad or happy. I think it was a combination of gratitude for being there with my folks, and grief for what I had lost physically since the last Thanksgiving. Dinner tasted like real food and I was thankful.

It was right about this time I felt anger toward God. I spent the week processing why my prayers hadn't been answered. I still had faith, but I was clearly disappointed with the outcome. I had to remind myself God did have a plan that may require the path I was on. He had the power to miraculously make everything go away, but He had decided to not intervene in the way I wished.

On November 28, I walked alone to my mailbox for the first time. It felt great to get outside, but I was pretty nervous and always had my cane nearby. Twenty-five days after surgery, I was walking outside.

My right arm continued to be weak. Writing slowly improved, and I was able to write my own checks again. I stopped taking narcotics to manage the pain. I was still experiencing intense head pain but found narcotics weren't helping much. I transitioned to regular doses of Tylenol and Motrin.

The end of November came. I received the bill from Mayo and found it quite interesting. I wanted people to know that despite my physical limitations, my mind was still sharp. I thought it might be entertaining to do some analysis. So I created a graph for my blog. I analyzed the hospital bill and saw some items listed that seemed a bit unusual and interesting. From what I could tell, my brain surgery experience had been a mere $85,000.

- craniotomy suboccip
- craniotomy exc of brain tumor, cerebellopontine ang (this is the long way to spell acoustic neuroma)
- screw micro auto-drive 1.6 x 4 m, 4 units (What's with Auto-drive??)
- plate ostemed str med 2 hole, 2 units (Do I still have two plates in my head? Wasn't one enough?)
- absorbable gelatin sponge, 2 each, 1 unit (I hope that has absorbed by now or I'll be accused of having a spongy brain, accurately.)
- resp svc resuscitation bag (If they used this, I didn't hear about it.)
- router fluted 1.85 x 16 m (I don't really want to know.)
- bur ball diamond 2m (I assume this is a drill bit.)
- bur acorn fluted 6m
- ball diamond 3.5 mm ext (How many drill bits does it take? Does this imply I am hard-headed?)
- probe mono prass std w/lead (What probing question could I ask here?)
- use of operating microscope, 4 units (I sure hope they could see well!! Two were for the surgeons, two for surgical assistants.)

- suture vicryl, 2 units
- suture vicryl (8), 2 units
- suture silk (8), 3 units (I am happy to hear things were tightly closed up when they were done!!)
- brainstem evoked potential (I don't even know what to say to this item.)

I continued to spend my days puttering around the house. Cautiously descending and ascending stairs, kind of cooking simple meals, and holding a heating pad to my face and head. Heat relaxed my muscles, which alleviated facial tightness and neck tension. I was watching the calendar for milestones as I felt my body slowly heal. Watching for the time when I would have to return to work. Watching for any sign of facial improvement. Wishing for any decrease in headaches. Before long, it had already been one month.

Chapter 17

Two Steps Forward, One Step Back

At one month, I was continuing to see steady (but slow) improvement. My head hurt less, and I could get up from a chair and walk further before I had to stop for a few seconds of brain freeze. I would experience a throbbing of my brain with a full spasm of my head and neck muscles, and termed it "waiting for my brain to catch up." I no longer used a cane to get around but continued to have poor balance. I was expecting more improvement after one month, but started to learn to adjust to my new status and changing timeline.

I was continuing to receive great comments from people on my blog. It was great reinforcement. While isolated in my house, it was great to know there were people watching and offering words of support.

I started to seek out help to speed up my healing. I started to go for regular massages with Mary, the therapist who I had seen as a gift before surgery. It felt incredibly good. One of her specialties is cranial sacral massage, which focuses on the flow of spinal fluid around your brain and through your spine. It seemed to release much of the anesthesia in my system. For the first time, I didn't feel nauseous. For the first time, I felt control over my bladder and its reluctance to function. I was able to go without having to concentrate and think about it.

Kayla had urged me to call my psychologist, Judy, because she didn't know how to help me with the strong emotions I was feeling. When I mentioned I wished the surgeons had just hit my brain stem and ended it all, she felt I needed help. I wasn't suicidal, but I was questioning what my quality of life was going to be. The pain was so intense from headaches that I didn't know how to cope.

I started to talk to Judy over the phone, as I didn't have the strength to drive to her office. She doesn't normally do counseling over the phone, but due to our long history, she agreed to give it a try. It was incredibly helpful.

Judy was as steady as a rock. She helped me sort out my feeling of anger toward God. We can't always know why God allows what He does, but we know He is there for us.

Judy helped me accept that we don't always get to find out why; we just have to have faith. She was helpful to me with finding value in my life. I was so used to being action and results oriented that I didn't know how to do nothing. She helped me accept that sometimes it is okay to just "be." It was okay to lay on the couch and spend time in prayer.

Lesson Learned

It's okay to just "be." We don't always have to be contributing to the world.

I started to do just that. I listened to music. I listened to audio books, but quickly abandoned that part of the plan when I kept falling asleep and missing entire chapters. I found it was peaceful to lie in one place with my eyes closed.

Kayla always seemed to be listening for any interest I showed to try something new. When I said I was interested in going Christmas shopping, she asked which day. She was spending one day a week with me, which we both enjoyed.

On December 5, at one month postsurgery, I went shopping for the first time. Kayla drove, and I got an electric wheelchair to conserve energy. It was a miracle I didn't run her over, but I eventually got the hang of it. A chair was the only hope of having enough energy to do anything outside the house. Walking the store at that point wasn't even an option for me. We had fun picking up miscellaneous Christmas gifts. (I had to get Kendra's box sent to France early.)

My eye bothered me nonstop that day. I couldn't get enough drops in it, and I couldn't keep it closed all the time. I complained to Kayla about it as I rubbed my eye. She repeatedly suggested I try some gel drops that I had read about, but I kept saying I didn't think it would make any difference and wouldn't be worth an extra stop at the drug store. Finally she just made the decision and turned into the drug store parking lot, where she went into the store and emerged with gel drops. I put them in my eye and found immediate and incredible relief. "Thanks Kayla, I guess they do make a difference."

Lesson Learned

Buy a lot of napkins and straws. If you have paralysis of your face, you will find eating to be a new challenge. It doesn't have to be a big deal if you prepare by having napkins and straws handy. Just learn to do what is necessary without explanation to others.

"If one thing doesn't work, it's time to try the next." We continued our day.

We went to a restaurant for lunch at one of my favorite places. Kayla ordered for me, and I ate slowly and deliberately using napkins excessively in my self-consciousness. Then I had a rest in the car while Kayla went to the pet store. I felt good enough though at the next stop to walk through the grocery store to pick up some frozen foods.

I had learned to keep my face emotionless so that the paralysis didn't seem as apparent. I developed a pattern where Kayla asked any questions I had so I wouldn't have to navigate the new world of single-sided deafness. In a quiet room I would hear fine, but as soon as any background noise was introduced, my brain became confused and hearing a person next to me was a challenge. My ears were ringing constantly, my head hurt, and my energy was low. However, I actually had fun. I had gotten out into the world and tasted normalcy.

Sometimes I felt like I updated the blog through rose-tinted glasses. I tend to be a people pleaser and was more concerned about the reader's comfort than sharing the tough parts of my journey. I joked that I made things sound so positive that people would be lining up for brain tumors! I told readers to understand that while I wanted them to celebrate progress with me; I realized I needed to share some of my struggles.

That Sunday was one of those bad days I expected. I felt I had experienced a great week, especially with getting out of the house to shop just two days earlier. However, Sunday hit like a brick wall. I got up and felt okay with a minimal headache. However, my head attacked at ten in the morning. I could barely get to the couch, as I had to stop every step for brain pain. I took a nap, assuming relief would follow. I woke up at 11:30 to even more pain. I knew food would help, but the kitchen seemed five miles away. I couldn't believe pain could be so intense that I couldn't move. However, it was real. I called my folks and cried, unable to get any words out other than, "Can you please come help?"

Within ten minutes, they were there springing into action. Dad warmed up some soup for me (that I couldn't eat), and Mom found pain medication for me. The pain was so severe that I clawed my way to the bathroom and threw up. The pain intensified, but eventually dulled with food and medication. I felt comforted by my folks' presence and support. Mom spent the night. Even at fifty-one years old, there's nothing like the love of parents and being fussed over.

Monday found me tired and weak, but back on track. I constantly reminded myself that tomorrow would bring another day. Where this path would lead I did not know, but I knew I still needed all the love, support, and prayers of my blog followers.

Day after day, I found getting up a little easier. It still took at least an hour. First I would get up and take Tylenol or Motrin. Then I would return to bed until the meds kicked in. Then I would take a long, hot shower that would help to relax my head and neck muscles.

I started to have lunch with my friends again. It was a good way to go somewhere and push myself while adjusting to my paralyzed face and headaches. They would pick me up initially when I was too weak to drive. I learned how to sit strategically to optimize my hearing by sitting with my good ear toward the waitress.

I was still in pain, but getting to know the new me. Slowly picking up the pieces of my life. Adjusting and accepting facial paralysis, which showed no sign of healing. I had lots of time on my hands to think, and try to figure out the meaning of life.

Chapter 18

The Philosopher Speaks

December 14, 2008

Life Lessons from the PETS

I have been home for quite some time now and have been observing the pet world. I would like to share what I've learned. Please note all quotations are from the pets. (Sorry, Kendra, I know that embarrasses you, but it is the most effective approach.)

1) Live for the moment - "What's up? Wanna lay down for a while? Okay," followed by nestling into the blankets as if for a lifetime. "What? You moved? Let me jump up just in case you wanted to go somewhere - the next room counts as going somewhere."

2) Life can change in an instant, be optimistic - "Let me outside! Really, it is important! Maybe it was snowing 5 minutes

ago, but it MIGHT be spring now. Really, I promise! If you get up off the couch and walk over here I'll go outside THIS time."

3) Sometimes you need a thick skin (From Gabby) - "I'm here! Let me lie on top of you with my whiskers in your face. OH, sorry, I know you didn't MEAN to push me off the bed. Here I am again in your face."

4) Sometimes our goals differ - We think we are on the same page but we aren't. We think we see things the same but we don't:

Gina: "Let me out—look at that!" while jumping excitedly at the door.

Paulo: "Just a minute, let me get out from under this blanket. Oh yea, I see it. Let me out too!!"

After both fitting out the door at the same time, they both run in different directions....

5) Unconditional Love - When I got home from Mayo, Gina jumped into my lap and quivered for about 20 minutes. She didn't care how bad I was feeling, she just wanted to be with me.

6) Sometimes there's nothing like a groan - Sometimes Paulo just groans. Well, since my surgery, I have groaned a lot! I have to admit it relieves pain and stress. Sometimes Paulo and I groan back and forth, which also provides comic relief!!

7) Sometimes things can serve two purposes - Gina constantly reminds me that I need to do "Right Hand" therapy … by petting her nonstop! It seems rather self-serving if you ask me.

December 15, 2008

My Omission

It was pointed out that I have pictures of Gina and Paulo (in the right column,) but none of Gabby. Here she is, in all her glory:

Of course, Paulo insisted on having his flattering blanket look featured. . . .

And Gina needed her regal pose posted ... a bit dark but that adds to the "mystery."

I was still resetting my vestibular system, as my balance was messed up by the surgery. I made great progress and learned to walk carefully as I continued to recalibrate. Sometimes I randomly veered to the left. One day at the grocery store, Kayla and I had two bags and a jug of milk. So when we headed out to the car, Kayla grabbed the bags and made a suggestion. Her suggestion was that if I carried the milk jug with my right hand, it would balance me and I wouldn't veer left randomly as much. Well, it worked. We laughed at the uniqueness of the "balance tool." We agreed the lesson for the day was "Sometimes you need to get a new tool or find a new use for an old one."

I enjoyed maintaining my blog and getting feedback in comments and e-mail. I found it fun to find various topics and have an audience for my rambling. Occasionally, I would remember something from my recovery that struck me funny. I would recap the experience on my blog. I strived for positive while realistic.

Lesson Learned

Learn to compensate for the new you. You may have to learn new ways to do certain things.

I got my first haircut. Once again I was humbled by how much people cared. Kris, my hair stylist, spent an hour and a half getting my hair cut just right. He shaped it and thinned the good side to match the surgery side. He refused money for it. Little things started to come together in my life. Slowly, but any kind of normalcy was welcome.

I was still pondering the purpose of the brain tumor. I was still struggling with God's plan for my life. I was, though, starting to see the world differently. People loved and gave, each in their own way. I was slowing down for the first time in fifty years, maybe to finally see some of what was always there.

Whenever I read my Bible or spent time in prayer, I always seemed to be hearing "Be Still. Wait on God."

"Really God? Haven't I been doing that?" I was impatient, but learning to be still in His presence. I was learning to depend on and appreciate others in my life. I was determined to listen to God and my body.

Chapter 19

Michigan Winter

December 23, 2008

Definition of REST (From Snowy Michigan)

It occurred to me, after being told to "rest" a lot, maybe I didn't really know the definition. SO, here it is. I think is a good word to review occasionally. I'm still working on the implementation of "rest" ... but trying and succeeding a bit.

REST: noun

1: repose, sleep; specifically: a bodily state characterized by minimal functional and metabolic activities

2 a: freedom from activity or labor; b: a state of motionlessness or inactivity; c: the repose of death

3: a place for resting or lodging

4: peace of mind or spirit

5 a (1): rhythmic silence in music; (2): character representing such a silence; b: brief pause in reading

6: something used for support

— at rest

1: resting or reposing especially in sleep or death

2: quiescent, motionless

3: free of anxieties

(ref: Merriam-Webster Dictionary Online) http://www. merriam-webster.com/dictionary/rest

I return to Mayo for my Three Month Checkup! on February 17. I will make an effort to REST until then and am dedicated to getting as good a report at that point as I can (BTEP Milestone?) One Milestone will be to see an MRI that is tumor free. I am feeling better all the time and instead of my energy going into "existence" my energy is now going toward building strength and trying to "rest."

Status check: It has now been 7 weeks since surgery.

Walk: I now walk pretty well. Still slow, but straighter and more confident. I have managed to not fall :)

Head pain: My head hurts less now (headache instead of frozen with pain).

Hearing in one ear: I find that living with hearing loss is mixed. In a quiet setting I'm fine. But the more background noise, the harder it is to distinguish what I want to hear.

Face: the muscles seem to be slowly strengthening, but there is a long way to go.

Chocolate: Yes! It tastes good again.

Attitude: I am grateful to be here and I do love life. It did sink in at some point that this really was a BRAIN tumor and I'm

lucky to be alive and have my intellect intact. The physical stuff is just a project that provides great opportunity for improvement.
HAPPY HOLIDAYS!!!

They said at Mayo the best physical therapy is just living normal life. So, I decided my physical therapy would incorporate shopping and eating out. I told some friends I would be open to going out to lunch, they said "How about Friday?" and we went. Just the activity of walking to the car, walking into the restaurant, talking to the waitresses, and adjusting to the various noises in the restaurant were providing great physical therapy!! As well as a sober reminder of how much further I had to go. I thought ahead to the feeling of accomplishment I'd have when I would no longer get dropped at the restaurant door. I thought ahead to doing my own driving.

At seven weeks, I walked around one neighborhood block. Margie came over to walk the dogs, and I wanted to go along, so I bundled up and off we went into the snow. Margie had to handle all three dogs (Gina, Paulo, and her dog Chester) and asked me how far—and I said around the block. *And* I made it. When we got back, Margie asked me how far I had made it prior to that walk. I said "the property line." Her eyes widened—she had had no idea and immediately felt guilty about taking me so far. It felt great. I slept well that night.

Christmas was fresh with the same lights hung in the neighborhood each year sprinkled with a renewed appreciation for life. I had Kayla bring my Charlie Brown Christmas tree up from the basement. Simple, green and a bit tacky with one large goldfish ornament. A tradition I had started several years ago with the girls. I was grateful. I appreciated lights, music, and the celebration of Christ's birth. I wasn't using the cane inside much, but I did use it when walking in the snow. My fear of falling was stronger than any confidence in my balance.

Chapter 20

The New Year Arrives

My lunch trips with friends proved to be great therapy. It was awkward to be in public with half of my face paralyzed. I moved slowly in an attempt to minimize aggravation to my constant head pain. I always rose from chairs cautiously and deliberately. Even then my brain would seize in pain for a minute before I could begin walking. It was hard to adjust to single-sided deafness, but I didn't like being home alone all the time. I pushed myself; I enjoyed the company.

In early January I faced the fact I would not be able to return to work after three months. I started the process of filing for disability. I was surprised at how emotionally difficult

Lesson Learned

Recognize that the new you is not the old you. Explain briefly to people if you have a limitation, like, "I'm sorry, but I can't hear on that side."

it was for me to admit I was disabled. It was hard to say the words to my boss. "I'm not going to be able to return yet. I have to file for disability." I was hoping if my body was given a few months more to rest it would get me to 100%. I couldn't accept it was more than a delay and assumed I would be back by fall. I would learn otherwise.

January 12, 2009

Philosophical Musings

I've had a lot of time to ponder over the last couple months. And I've talked with many of my friends and family about the proverbial bus that ran over me. I don't have any answers (and probably won't) but have considered the following:

God. Yes, I have wondered why the prayers of a miracle haven't been answered—I guess He felt I was strong enough to tough it out (by the way, I disagree :)). However, it did occur to me that God provided for my unknown needs without prayer. He helped prepare the setting before I even knew I had a brain tumor. There are incredible stories behind each that are too long to tell here.

1. I moved from Princeton to Michigan.
2. My parents live 2 miles away.
3. Kayla and Mark moved to Michigan. Kayla decided to not get a job right away while she finished her MBA.
4. Kendra happened to be here for a couple days when I got the tumor diagnosis.
5. Insurance - I have great health insurance and got a disability policy two years ago.

Bottom line, the lesson for today is, "God knows what's coming and knows of our need even before we do and He prepares the path for us while we live in oblivion. So why is it so hard to trust Him to decide what's the best answer for our current prayers?"

I grappled with the big word "disability." I would later walk on the ocean shore in Florida and marvel at the word and its misconceptions. Once again, I would take to my computer to capture how I was feeling. I tried to capture life's dilemmas.

In human nature, we have a tendency for fight or flight. I like flight. I like to soar from issues like a seagull floating through the blue, cloudless sky. Fighting is clingy and exhausting like feet stuck in sucking, wallowing muck. Fighting feels like being cornered by giants.

A significant life change requires "coming to terms with" or "learning to live with." That comes with becoming disabled. Living with. Living and not dying. Not able. Not complete. I find myself internally screaming that I am still me. I remember what smiling felt like, spreading across my entire face from ear to ear with the apples of my cheeks pushing up into my eyes with delight. I remember surround sound, entering both ears in a circle that can't be understood until it is only half there. I remember what headache free felt like, light with continuous energy flowing through my head. Disabled means losing, not forgetting. Disabled means partial, not complete. Disabled means incomplete; yet a complete heartache.

Becoming disabled is terrifying, seeing your life fall off a cliff. Not knowing how far down—or not. At first it was dark and tight. I couldn't think about how far I'd fallen because it took all effort just to breathe. I lay, panting, taking inventory at the dim base of the cavern. Eventually I could do more than just breathe and began to crawl to the cliff to climb. I slowly made progress. My family hovered at the top of the cliff. Their cheers varied from pity to tough love. "You poor thing." "It is what it is, right?"

Sometimes I fall back, crashing on a ledge. I haven't fallen as far as the bottom, but I've lost ground. Once again I am breathless for a period. Eventually I start climbing again. I've been told I'll never reach the top again but I still climb, knowing, hoping, praying the next ledge will feel just a little closer to normal; feel a little closer to the old me. Not wanting to accept "the new me," a phrase used in the disability world. Hearing the phrase sounds like something someone else should deal with. It takes time, lots of time, to accept it is not just a phrase, but a whole new identity I myself need to accept. It means I really won't ever be the "old me" again. That is a big concept to swallow. It is a concept I haven't swallowed yet.

The calm after a storm. My head after a bad day when I haven't been able to do more than get from the bed to the couch. Sore, exhausted, panting like muscles after a workout. Pain following pain. Still, tired pain. Residual pain. I am thankful in all things. Pain reminds me in its intensity that I am not always in that much pain. In its intense moments I am thankful for life and for good moments I can draw upon. Disability is constant. Disability doesn't stop.

Lesson Learned

Accept that the future you is still undefined. Recovery takes time.

Disability doesn't mean the absence of pleasure or the absence of life. It doesn't mean stopping. Disability is still being alive and able to do new things. Disability draws focus to things that may have gone unnoticed before. I was learning, day by day, what it meant to move on with my life when disabled.

Chapter 21

Waiting for Healing

Sudden deafness in one ear was strange. Hearing was essentially normal at times and agonizing at others. I was adjusting. At first, I would feel but not hear water on my head in the shower. I would scratch my head to silence. At about three months, I started to "hear" those things on the right side. So was I really hearing them? I was puzzled. Through research I learned about bone conduction. As the nerves healed on my scalp I was able to hear scratching as it was transmitted through my bone of my skull to the left ear.

I was frustrated overall with my healing. I saw improvement, but it was a long and slow incline. I learned to be grateful for any improvement. I was grateful to still be alive, even if trudging along. I thanked God for my life. One moment I would be okay with "being still" and then turn around and feel restless and frustrated. It was a continual battle of wills. All moot as my head dictated what I did and didn't do.

In late January, I decided to try flying in a plane for the first time. I considered it to be for research purposes (i.e., would my head explode? And for the record, no, it didn't). I scheduled a direct flight from Kalamazoo to Orlando to spend a week with Nancy and her husband Randy. Dad dropped me at the Kalamazoo airport (5 degrees Fahrenheit) and they picked me up in Orlando (77 degrees Fahrenheit). The flight was okay, but exhausting. Nancy had a heating pad waiting for me, and I alternated walking outside and napping. It was a great break from the Michigan winter, and a new surrounding for my continued recovery.

I enjoyed the warmer weather of Florida. We walked on the beach. I took pictures. They caught me when I tipped over. We sat when my head hurt, surrounded by the heating pad. When returning to the airport, it was all I could do to contain the pain in my head to push forward and get home.

Part of my push to fly was the uncertainty of my future. I was in the process of filing for disability insurance. How long would I need it? I was concerned about what I was going to do for a living. I really didn't know if I would be able to return to my consulting job.

It was a successful trip. Successful in telling me I was far from ready for anything beyond pain medication and naps. Michigan was cold. My headaches were back with a vengeance. I wondered if weather had any relationship to my pain.

In February, I learned that brain surgery was nothing compared to filling out disability paperwork. Claims people are sharply different from sales people, who are friendly and supportive when selling you a policy. Detail-oriented claims people were pleasant but thorough and distrustful. I filled out several sets of forms, and we waited for records from everywhere and anywhere to confirm I didn't already know about the brain tumor when I took out my disability policy. I hunted down doctors to obtain statements. None of us knew how long I would be disabled, but it was clear I wasn't ready to return to work. I was torn emotionally between appreciating the financial support and disappointment with reality. Initially, I sought a few months of disability for healing, building strength, and getting my headaches under control. Later I would find that a few months were not enough. I was setting the groundwork for my future. I was setting the groundwork for retirement.

Warmer spring weather arrived. I was able to get out and walk more. I was able to walk outside without a cane, so I referred to the cane as totally "yesterday." I still veered randomly but didn't tip over. In early February, I walked my dogs for the first time. I was learning to trust my balance when not on snow and ice. Kayla was right there to provide any needed assistance. While I managed to control both my body and two dogs, I knew it would be quite a while before I was able to confidently walk my dogs.

I frequently read posts out on the Acoustic Neuroma Association web site. One post asked people to write about the "new me" we were all experiencing. I pondered that question, and summarized my current status with this:

> I am now at three months. I am evolving and trying to be patient while my body determines what the "new me" will be. I am fluctuating between hope for an improved outcome over time and striving for acceptance of what may not improve.
>
> I am amazed at the broad range of outcomes that are experienced with AN Surgery—from practically skipping out of the hospital to life-changing effects. I did a lot of research prior to my surgery, but still felt unprepared for

my outcome. I think the reality was an outcome I was totally in denial about as an even remote possibility. The hearing and the balance weren't terribly "visible." However, losing my beautiful smile with a yet unknown outcome has been very hard and difficult to even comprehend. I hate seeing someone I know for the first time because it is such an immediate expression of sympathy and awkwardness. I'm trying to adjust my thinking to considering all these new "features" to be badges of honor that allow me to "flaunt" that I survived brain surgery! (Sometimes it actually works)

The headaches are also hard to understand. I have different headaches every day. I hope it is still the healing process. Randomly, when I get up from sitting down, I have "brain freezes" after taking a few steps. I have learned to just stop and stand while they slowly release. "Never be in a hurry" is my motto. Sometimes the back of my head hurts. Sometimes my brain throbs inside my skull. If I drop something on the floor I debate how important it is to pick it up and leave stuff on the floor for days until I feel up to dealing with the head pain of bending down to pick it up. How to describe the levels of pain to a headache neurologist seems daunting. (I will be seeing one later this month.) I guess I'm trying to decide what to just "suck up" and what to try to address with drugs or therapy.

Given all of that, I'm incredibly grateful to be alive and to have retained all that I did. I am humbled at how kind everyone in my life has been. Thanks for starting this thread. I think it feels good to just vent and contemplate as we try to describe the difference between the old and new.

Chapter 22

Return to Mayo at Three Months

inally, the date came for my three month checkup. It was depressing and encouraging. The doctors were incredibly supportive and equally disappointed with my status. However, they encouraged me by predicting the pain would subside. I learned several things:

My MRI was clear enough that I didn't need another for at least a year. Images showed the tumor is gone, although it left an interesting dent in my brain. They were confident it will not return as it was an acoustic tumor and the hearing nerve was removed along with the tumor, leaving nothing for it to grow on. I learned that Mayo has 26 MRI machines. I was amazed.

The hearing nerve was GONE. It was tangled with a critical blood vessel, and too mangled to save. It was interesting to hear the brain surgeon talk through the logic of decisions during surgery.

The facial nerve was intact. However, it was weak from the beginning of surgery, so it was almost ready to go even without surgery. It was good to know—kind of—that I would have had some degree of facial paralysis even without surgery. The tumor was growing and stretching the nerve. We could see a little squiggle on the MRI that showed the still out of shape (not straight) nerve.

Nerve recovery requires the nerve to regenerate all the way, not just where it was traumatized, so from the brain out to the face. So my initial calculations were short when I thought that only the little damaged section inside my skull needed to heal. Nerves regenerate at a rate of 1mm a day, so I recalculated that it would be six to eighteen months, at least, before my facial nerve would fully recover.

They did believe my face would recover to some extent. According to House-Brackmann ratings, a score that grades the degree of nerve damage, facial movement is rated One through Six, with One being normal and Six no movement. The measurement is determined by measuring the upwards movement of the mid-portion of the top of the eyebrow, and the outwards movement of the angle of the mouth. I was currently a Six. Dr. Driscoll predicted I would become a Two or Three when all is said and done. That would be not fully normal, but definitely moving. Dr. Link thought my face looked tighter, which is the beginning of healing.

The right hand surprised everyone. They didn't have any idea why I couldn't write. Link said he thought it was trauma from the tumor being stuck to the brain stem. It was still improving but wasn't there yet.

I met a wonderful headache neurologist, Dr. Cutrer. He was a Southern gentleman who I liked right away as he swept into the examining room. He sat down at a desk and just talked. "Did you have headaches before brain surgery?"

"No," I replied.

"Well then, we don't have to try to figure out what caused them, do we? It seems to be common for some craniotomy patients to have long-term headaches. We don't really know why, but we know it happens. I am keeping a database of all my patients to track what works and what doesn't. I want to work with you to get rid of them and am confident we can."

I was so relieved to hear his commitment I thought I might cry. I was expecting the usual doctor dismissal of pain. I immediately dropped all my defenses. I wondered why they don't know more, but before I asked, it occurred to me that in the past, a brain tumor meant death. It hasn't been that many years that people have survived brain surgery!

He continued, "I want you to use a three tier approach to your head pain. I want you to take an antidepressant, amitriptyline, daily because we have had great luck with headache relief from them. Once you are up to full strength it should knock out background, steady pain. If you get up and don't feel great, you go to number two, Ketoprofen. It is the big bad cousin of Motrin. If two hours later you are still in pain, then you go to drug number three, Maxalt, which is a migraine medication."

I was grateful to have a doctor who understood. The charming Southern doctor said, "It is always good to have a couple extra arrows in your quiver for whatever pain you may have. If these don't work, I've got more drugs we can try. Don't try to be a hero. If it hurts, take something."

I asked a few questions and left feeling hopeful for the first time since surgery. As I walked out with multiple prescriptions and sheets of instructions, he closed with, "Give me a call when you have a headache-free day. I look forward to being fired as your headache doctor!"

I met with a vestibular therapist. He tested my balance. Overall, I felt my balance was pretty good. However, I still couldn't type on my Blackberry while walking. But I learned that my eyes were doing a lot of my balancing. When I closed my eyes, I tipped over when standing still with my feet together. So he gave me some simple exercises to get my brain out of the "panic" mode when walking and moving.

I finished my visit with a visit to their photographer, who pinned my hair back and took pictures of my face in various expressions. I knew that the pictures were far from glamour shots, showing each detail of my dysfunction. I was self-conscious, but it was obvious that nothing phased the skilled medical photographer.

After returning to my hotel, I updated my blog and expressed my appreciation. Once again, I gave prayer instructions. For those who wanted complex directions, I asked that they pray for the facial nerve to heal and for headache management with minimal side effects from drugs. I posted MRI images from before surgery and at three months postop.

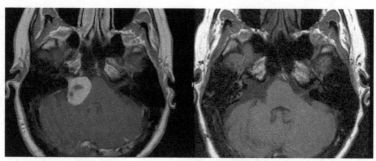

Before Sep '08   **After Feb '09**

Chapter 23

A Typical Day
with Headaches

Each morning, I would awaken, and be still for a minute. I would feel rested and content if I had had several continuous hours of sleep. I would slowly stretch and turn my head on the pillow, all in drowsy gratitude. Suddenly, as my head turned, it would be struck with pain faster than a cobra's attack. My eyes would pop open. My neck would feel stiff and the whole right side of my head would tighten. There's nothing like a postcraniotomy headache. It was going to be a bad head day. There was randomness regarding how I would feel at any time.

On those days, my brain felt raw inside my skull as if there was no padding between my brain and skull. Nature provides padding through cerebrospinal fluid that flows around the brain and spinal cord, but it felt like I was running on empty those mornings. As soon as I moved, I also had two delighted pets clamoring for attention, crawling over my body, immune to my pain. "Not now, guys," I would say as I pushed them away. They backed off, but watched expectantly, waiting for my next move. Gabby loved to sleep on my chest. Gina loved to be petted. Paulo slept; an immobile bump under the covers. It would take dynamite to wake that little Italian Greyhound.

After taking a few slow breaths, I'd slowly ease out of bed, placing my feet firmly on the floor, raising my head and body in slow motion. I'd sit for a minute and breathe steadily. I'd stand up, and then still, waiting for my balance to adjust to the new day. Once I thought it was safe, I'd head toward the bathroom. If I moved too fast my brain halted any further progress for a few seconds while I waited for brain freeze to release—like when you drink something cold too fast, times ten. I was learning to live with what is called "Wonky Head" by acoustic neuroma patients.

Like a drunkard, I'd head to the bathroom, feeling like I had an incredible hangover. Surgery had destroyed my balance system, atrophying my right cerebellum, requiring my brain to recalibrate itself in the morning. Between the bed and bathroom, like pinball in slow motion, I'd touch my dresser to the left, the wall to the right and then stop, gripping the bathroom door jamb with both hands. Touching things made me feel more grounded. Slowly, I'd lower myself to the toilet. I'd smiled to myself cynically. Many people pay to feel bad when they over-drink. I only have to get out of bed to feel bad. I'm slowly rise and take my tier one medication to get the day started.

Gina, my morning dog, always rolls on my bedroom carpet, scratching her little grey back as she waits for me. Emerging from the bathroom, I'd find her eagerly greeting me with her tail wagging wildly, always as happy to see me as if I had been gone a week instead of two minutes. Paulo, not a morning dog, would still be an immobile lump under the covers. Down the stairs I'd go with Gina right by my side for the slow descent.

"Meow," Gabby complained as she lumbered behind us down the stairs. She is a bit portly, so her footsteps are louder than the dog's delicate greyhound steps. Evidently her food bowl was empty.

With Gina outside, I'd stand and look out the patio door, trying to appreciate the Michigan morning. Weather changes could be one reason for such a bad head day. I am quite sure the doctors inserted a barometer in my skull after they opened it with their fancy diamond drill bit. I'd hold my head, as if it would help. I had to eat something with my morning drugs, so I'd move slowly to the cupboard to get a pain pill and mix a protein shake.

"MEOW!!"

"Yes, Gabby," I said, "I'm coming with your breakfast." Her Siamese meow was more plaintive than polite. Maybe we should have named her something quieter.

I'd let Gina back in and feed her. That required me to get a half cup of food from a standing height to her bowl on the floor without bending my raw head, so I'd tip the scooper toward her bowl from a slightly bent position. "There you go, Gina. Most of it hit your bowl!" Pieces fell in or near her bowl.

Then it was back up the stairs to bed. I'd groan as I lowered my head to the pillow. From somewhere under the covers, Paulo groaned back. He'd wiggle to the top of the bed and lick behind my ear where the craniotomy scar is. People claim dogs can tell when you've had trauma. I wouldn't disagree. He'd lick behind my ear only on the tumor side; more frequently when he could tell I was in pain. Too bad it didn't help.

Eventually I'd drag myself back up and take my morning shower. I was hoping the hot water would relax my head. Some mornings it didn't. I'd slowly dress without bending or allowing my head to drop below my heart. The resulting head pain would have caused me to return to bed for at least a half hour. If I dropped my hairbrush on the floor, I'd stare at it like it was a hundred miles away. *It isn't worth it to bend for.* I'd get out another brush. The first brush could stay on the floor until a better day. I'd reach for Ketoprofen, my tier two drug.

I'd head back down the stairs, always with two dogs following me. Paulo would have finally gotten up. I'd sit down at my computer, needing to write. Even though I had a good excuse not to. Sometimes nothing would come to mind except how much my head hurt. So that's what I would write.

After a couple hours, if my head still hadn't released, I'd return to the cabinet for my third tier pain pill. I might remember the conversation I had with the Dr. Cutrer, the headache neurologist at Mayo Clinic. "Give me a call when you have a headache-free day. I look forward to being fired as your headache doctor!" Now, months later, I'd mutter to myself as I swallowed drug number three, "When will that happen, doc?" I have yet to experience a full day without headaches. I'd give myself the usual pep talk: "You could have died. How's that for an alternative? You're alive, aren't you?"

Lesson Learned

Accept that there will be good and bad days—learn to gauge your activities on how you feel, not how you want to feel.

A half hour later, I'd felt my head relaxing. I didn't take it for granted. I was ready to take on and enjoy the rest of my day. For my brain's sake, I sure hoped to not sneeze or cough! Of course, an afternoon nap would be payment for the Maxalt. But who's complaining?

The next morning I would awaken and cautiously move. Maybe it would be tolerable pain on that day. "Today will be a good head day!" I'd say to myself, smiling. A good day would mean at least a few hours of minimal pain if I remained fairly inactive. I had learned to appreciate lesser pain and short periods of feeling good. Perhaps I would feel up to picking up that hairbrush today.

Chapter 24

Moving Forward and Rejoining Life

One very cold winter day in March, at four months postsurgery, I made it back to Al Sabo Land Preserve. Kayla, Mark, Paulo, and Gina all bundled up with me, and off we went on a frigid sunny day! There was a lot of ice on the walking path, so it was slow going. But it was great to get out into nature again. My doctors would have been happy because I was walking on uneven ground—a good workout for balance.

On another sunny Sunday in March, Kayla and Mark came over, and we went to Milham Park. It was a great opportunity for another vestibular workout. And the dogs discovered geese. Good thing they were on leashes, or Paulo would have gone right in after them!! It was good to get my camera out again and start taking beautiful nature and landscape pictures.

While I loved my new freedom of going out into warmer and warmer weather, I was disappointed to not have my headaches letting up. I was continuing to increase my daily dose of amitriptyline, but I still needed the other drugs almost daily.

At five months, I got a call from my Kalamazoo friend Nancy, who invited me to travel to Florida with her family for a week in April. I obviously had nothing going on, so I quickly said yes, how soon? It was a great week with little stress. I rode down with them and quickly settled into the routine of sleep and relaxation. I was disappointed that my headaches were still quite severe and limited my ability to walk or participate in activities. At least I had a different and pleasant view out the window.

One day Nancy and I stopped by the pool bar to order lunch. Music blared, assaulting my new single-sided deafness. I decided to barrel through though, so when the waitress asked me a question I didn't hear, I assumed I knew what she was asking. I answered that I wanted to put lunch on my Visa. The girl looked at me. Nancy started laughing. "She asked if you want fries with your burger."

"Oh, oops. Yes, fries please." It was the first time I hadn't wanted to cry when confused with my hearing. Having Nancy laugh made me realize it actually was kind of funny and I could laugh too. It wasn't the end of the world.

Lesson Learned
Learn to laugh at yourself. It will help you to feel less self-conscious.

While in Panama City, we walked on the beach every day. I slowed Nancy and Steve down, and couldn't go far, but it was great to be outside moving again. My balance was challenged as I walked along the uneven shore. I found I was constantly listing to the right. When I had walked as much as possible for the day, I'd encourage Nancy to continue walking and I'd head back alone. "No way. I'm not going to tell your family I let you walk alone and you veered into the ocean." We'd laugh and turn back together, Nancy walking between me and the ocean.

Head pain was severe and forced me to bed quite early each night. It was worth the difficulties to be around friends. My face, still immobile on the right side, made me feel self-conscious when meeting people. Nancy's family and friends accepted me and made me feel human again.

April 8, 2009

Very Uneven Ground

Well, this week finds me in Panama City Beach, Florida, with my friend Nancy P. and her family. They had room for a stowaway when they drove down, so I was in. I have been focusing on my vestibular rehabilitation while down here. That requires a lot of walking on the beach. Whenever I am done with a walk, I need to rest my vestibular system. I am doing that by resting by the pool in the sun (vitamin D infusion). I think it is working!

April 11, 2009

Spring Break '09

That was a fast week. We are back in Michigan. We had a great time in Florida, although I certainly felt old with all the young people converging for Spring Break.

I struggle to describe my current status. I feel pretty good a lot of the time and am able to manage my headaches most of the time. I am no longer constantly feeling overwhelming pain, which now comes in spikes. The headaches are clearly still in control of my life. It is unpredictable when I will have a good day or a bad one. The daily drugs are not up to full strength for another month or two, but do seem to be minimizing the steady background pain. I am just trying to enjoy and appreciate life around the challenging times, and breathe a lot and take extra drugs when they do come.

I've become fascinated with taking pictures of birds in flight. They frequently do not cooperate, even though Nancy and Steve can attest to the fact that I did ask the birds nicely. They fly the wrong way, they refuse to fly, or they fly too fast to snap the shot. Despite their lack of cooperation, here's one that turned out pretty good.

For some silly reason, Nancy convinced me to have my picture taken. She suggested that if we both held our smiles, nobody would know my facial nerve hasn't healed yet. We were laughing so hard it took several attempts. I think this week helped me learn to laugh at the challenges of the new me.

The meadow at Al Sabo was now green with spring growth. I had made the full circle of seasons with the nature preserve. I thought about how much had changed in one short year. Less than a year ago, walking in budding spring and summer in full bloom, I had no knowledge of a brain tumor. Now, as spring and summer returned, I was amazed to think about how far I had come. Not far enough to be back to my normal life, but feeling pretty good a reasonable amount of the time.

In May, at six months, I was almost up to full strength on my headache medication, amitriptyline. I had been working up since February, 10 mg a week with a break in the middle. I had learned that when you are dealing with the brain you need to be conservative for some reason—go figure. I looked forward to my patience being rewarded when the medication kicked in sometime in the next month or two. Relief from the headaches that were still a part of my daily life was overdue in my humble opinion! As my wise mother used to say, "Enough is enough, and I've had enough." However, I still had no relief.

I was appreciating life though, considering the alternative. I seemed to finally be learning to take one day at a time. I was getting out for a walk most days. Some days were good, and some were terrible. While it is true I didn't exactly get a vote in the matter, I started to learn to appreciate slowness. I don't think I have ever, in my life, done anything slowly. I didn't realize it was an option, and I was finding there was something to be said for it.

I did learn some valuable lessons from months without movement in my face, with no promise for the future. One was regarding pictures and vanity. I was in my daughter's wedding pictures a couple years prior, and I had been stressed about how fat I looked in the mother-of-the-bride dress. I looked past my beautiful smile without even thinking about it or appreciating it. At the time, Kendra told me I shouldn't be down on myself because we are all beautiful in different packages. (Wise young woman.) What is really interesting is that my favorite picture was of me hugging my daughter and all you can see is the back of my head! My favorite picture, which brings me great memories, doesn't even have my fully functioning face in it.

Now what I missed most was my smile, and I could have kicked myself for being so silly about a few pounds in the past. My daughters always remind me that I am still me, even with half a smile. It is better to have all of my life memories than to have lost who I am. So it was hard to be in pictures, but when big moments come, I'll be right there celebrating life with my family. I will be creative with my posing to try to show the joy half of my face can still show. (Glass half full theory.) I won't deny the joy of the moment to avoid a picture.

In the hospital, I'm sure my family left the room to cry at times, but they never showed me anything but strength, love, and support. I was watching them for reactions to gauge how horrified I should be myself. With their acceptance, I got through it.

ANs help us with life perspectives. I believe AN survivors are grateful and well-grounded people who would probably do it all again even with the individual challenges and outcome if it was the price to spend life with our loved ones.

Chapter 25

One Tiny Movement

O n June 4, my face started to smile. That morning, I looked in the mirror as I did every morning, searching my face for any improvement. I couldn't believe it when I saw a slight twitch at the corner of my mouth. It was a tiny movement as my lips started to turn up a bit in the right corner, but my heart leaped. I proudly told my family, who failed to see it. They humored me with encouragement until more movement returned over the following weeks. It's hard to describe the emotional boost I got from that tiny movement. It was a huge relief to know the process had started.

In June, I wrapped up my blog. I felt I needed to make one last entry to let people know. I still got e-mail from people who were disappointed that I ended it. My expectations were exceeded with the success of my blog.

June 12, 2009

The End. . . for now

I can't believe it has been a month since I've updated this blog! I have decided it is time to wrap it up. My updates are few and far between and becoming redundant. For anyone still reading, thanks. I have gotten amazing feedback.

I am still here, but stuck in a bit of a Groundhog Day scenario. I still have headaches, and will be going back to Mayo in August for my next checkup. The headache neurologist there is working with me, but it takes forever to get up to full dose on a medication that may not work. So I'm hanging in here, but still hanging :)

Thanks to everyone!!

In July, at about eight months I was still having daily headaches. I started to really be discouraged by it. Starting, you say? Yes, for the first six months I just assumed it was "normal" and would decrease over time. It hadn't despite months of ramping up my dosage of amitriptyline. I needed Ketoprofen and Maxalt almost every day and was limited on Maxalt to eighteen a month due to insurance limitations. I was still on disability.

The problem with headaches is that unspoken, "How bad can it be? Just suck it up and go on." Well, I tried to tell myself that. Sometimes I got so frustrated I'd just barrel through something I used to be able to do (like look up to change batteries in my smoke detectors or walk my dogs). I then paid for it either by being unable to complete the task due to my head, or I had a terrible next day. So much for my pontificating about the wonderful lessons I had learned through this process. I was running out of patience.

I went for a walk one day with Margie. It was a beautiful summer day, and I looked forward to getting out and spending time with my friend. My head hurt quite a bit that day, but I willed it to settle with walking. It got steadily worse. I tried to ignore it but it screamed at me. I slowed, and eventually froze. I sat on the curb and was immobilized by pain. Margie suggested waving down a passing UPS truck for a ride back to my house, but I passed. After a few minutes of hopelessness, I mustered my strength, breathed deeply, stood, and walked straight home. I collapsed on the couch and didn't move for hours.

When I got a periodic call from the disability company I would feel incredible guilt that I hadn't been able to go back to work. I had to admit though, that I was unable to function normally in any capacity. I would love to have passed on the brain tumor and subsequent issues, but I never got a vote. Then I would cycle through anger that I allowed myself to feel guilty, and then sadness for the new me, and grief for the lost me.

On August 1, I checked in with my former client to update them on my status and to check in on how they were doing.

Greetings Folks,

For some reason, I woke up today and wanted to send you guys an update. Maybe because it has almost been a full year (in September) since I last saw you. My recovery has been so long and drawn out it makes me say "ARGH." But not with too much emphasis or my head will hurt! I know you guys really care, and since I stopped updating my blog, I thought I'd send a note. The blog started to bore even me. There are only so many ways to say "I walked my dogs today and my head still hurts."

The good news is that my facial nerves have started to regenerate. I almost have my whole smile back. I have to tell you when the right side of my face started moving I had a huge boost of encouragement. I really missed my smile and it is great to have it mostly back. I still have more healing to go, but I don't feel like a sagging stroke victim anymore.

The not-so-good news, or should I say old news is that my headaches are still a problem. In February, the headache neurologist at Mayo (which sounds pretty impressive to me) put me on a "miraculous" combination of "wonder" drugs I could "put in my quiver" to manage my headaches. They do give quite a bit of relief, but not until I have taken all three almost daily to relieve a headache that makes me feel like I have an arrow stabbing my skull. My articulate daughters describe my headaches as "crippling," and my father says, "Oh boy, they just don't stop, do they?" So far, the drugs are leaving me to wonder what the miracle is. It seems wondrous to me that my head still hurts after so long. I will be going back to Mayo in August and hope to find new arrows for my quiver.

So, I'm still here, just hanging out trying to be good natured about the whole thing. I hope all is well with you!! I hope the bad economy isn't hitting you too hard. You should have seen a spike in pharmaceutical consumption in the Southwest Michigan area. It is the least I could do.

Chapter 26

An Eye-Opening Symposium

August was a busy month. Kendra and I attended the ANA Symposium in Chicago. It is a conference dedicated to acoustic neuroma tumor education held every other year. We met many other patients, and it was great to find camaraderie with people who understood what I was going through. It was strange to be surrounded by people whose faces looked similar to mine in their dysfunction. There were also many people in the watch and wait category, gathering information. As my first outing into the real world, my head, hearing, and face would remind me of my new limitations.

The rooms were noisy. At the tables, it was awkward and almost comical that most people were deaf in one ear. That made positioning important to ensure that each could hear the table's conversation. My brain quickly reached overload, and I found myself retreating from the group sessions. My single-sided deafness was uncomfortable and frustrating.

We attended a session on facial retraining. It was fascinating as the speaker, Jackie Diels, explained synkinesis and how you could treat it through therapy. Synkinesis is when facial nerve fibers, after being torn or severed, implant or reconnect to the wrong nerve group. This causes undesired and simultaneous facial movements. The result is abnormal movement of facial muscles, or muscles other than those intended contract during a particular movement pattern. What? That means when you smile, your forehead raises. However, you may be unable to lift your forehead when giving your brain that specific command.

She also talked about how facial paralysis heals but transforms into muscle spasms which make one feel that there has been no improvement. Movements are impossible until the muscles are stretched and relaxed from a Charlie horse–like state that they move into after the facial nerve heals and the brain has been trying too hard to move. If it doesn't move one way, the brain tries for another, resulting in confusion and dysfunction—ultimately with tightened and immobile muscles. It was strange, but made sense. That explained why the standard look of a post-AN person is with their lip raised on one side as the tight cheek pulls up.

Following the session, Kendra encouraged me to approach Jackie to introduce myself and ask about my case. I had gotten her business card, but Kendra wasn't satisfied with that.

Lesson Learned
Each body, tumor, and outcome is unique.

She pushed me to actually talk to Jackie. She was an incredibly warm and energetic lady who encouraged me to come see her in Wisconsin for a personal session. She said the timing, with my facial nerve just starting to heal, would be perfect.

As the symposium continued, we went to sessions on headache management, and on hearing aid topics. We learned the only option for a person with no auditory nerve was a BAHA, a bone anchored hearing aid. A titanium post is permanently implanted in the skull, and the hearing aid is snapped on and off daily. It was all interesting. However, with my head already hurting I had no desire to have anything implanted in my skull. We learned about tinnitus, or ringing in the ears. I learned the reason I still had loud ringing despite no auditory nerve was because my brain was turning up the volume in an attempt to hear!

My headaches were still intense, but we managed to attend all of the sessions that we wanted. We had a nice mother-daughter time in Chicago unlike any other time that we had spent together. It was incredibly eye opening for Kendra, who had been in France during surgery.

We drove directly from Chicago to the Mayo Clinic where I had my nine-month check-up. The doctors were incredible, once again. My headaches were clearly still a mystery, and the doctors were supportive with my disability.

We spent the day going from appointment to appointment, although fewer and briefer than at three months. The surgeon was pleased to see some facial movement had returned. The headache neurologist changed my medication to Gabapentin. This would require a slow removal of amitriptyline and then buildup of the new drug. It was clear this was a long road, and this was one stop on what was to become a regular visit to Mayo through the years. I was nowhere near firing Dr. Cutrer. At nine months, I had not yet had one day without a headache.

Chapter 27

Addressing Facial Synkinesis

I n October 2009, at eleven months postsurgery, I went to Madison, Wisconsin, for facial retraining with Jackie Diels. It was amazing, with immediate results. Again I was in for a lesson in patience. I learned it would not be a one-time, one-visit fix. Facial therapy is a lifelong process. I spent three days with Jackie, who introduced me to neuromuscular facial retraining.

My brother went with me and hung out while I was in my appointments. The first day was educational. Jackie explained the anatomy of the face, synkinesis, and brain retraining. She studied my face and determined what I specifically needed to do. Her therapy is time consuming and individual. She explained that every case is different, so there is no "cookbook" for neuromuscular facial retraining.

She showed me that looking at a picture of ourselves in the mirror reflects what we are used to seeing every day. She explained that with facial muscles, small movement is good. We don't smile big except in pictures. Trying to force a muscle to work is not effective, and in fact will result in more abnormal function as the brain becomes determined to move the face. So, using an electrical impulse machine on a paralyzed face will actually cause more synkinesis. If a muscle is ready to move, and is relaxed without spasms, it will move. If not, no exercise will make a difference. Facial exercise is the opposite of any other muscle workout.

We spent most of the first day working on stretching and massaging my face. She asked if my face was painful or tight. No, not that I had noticed. However, when she had me start to press on areas of my cheek, it started to scream! After holding the tight muscles with my fingers inside and outside of my mouth, the muscle spasms relaxed and released their grasp on my face. It felt much better. The changes were even immediately visible in the mirror. My cheek relaxed and my mouth was less tight. When Al picked me up, he immediately saw the differences in my face. We were amazed.

That evening, I picked up a microwavable clay heating pack at the drugstore. I heated and applied it repeatedly through the evening and next morning. Heat assisted with the relaxation of my muscles. My face felt like a pummeled piece of meat.

The following two days were spent continuing to dig into my face and find where it was seized up and needed relaxing. Jackie introduced me to the concept of brain retraining, and how through concentration I could affect some of the movements of my face. She explained it to be like teaching yourself to wiggle your ears. Or to snarl only on one side, which many people have trouble with. I visualized a brick wall holding my face hostage and mentally broke the wall down, brick by brick. I focused my mind on how the left, normal side felt and tried to replicate the feeling and movement on the right. It was a mind game. A tough one I fight to this day.

October 21, 2009
Almost One Year

Greetings to anyone who still checks in here occasionally! I know newly diagnosed acoustic neuroma patients are occasionally finding this site, so I feel compelled to give an update!

I am still having headaches, and have been told it will be a long ride. After AN surgery, a small percentage of patients have long-term headaches. It seems to be due to damage to the dura, or the lining of the brain. Over time it is supposed to improve, but the time varies per individual. Headaches are still keeping me from working.

What I have learned through this journey is that each person has their own unique set of life-changing effects. Some are a bump in the road, and some make you feel like you were the bump run over repeatedly by a bus. However, it does get better! There is wonderful company and camaraderie on the ANA website: http://www.anausa.org/forum/. So if you are new to this, be sure to visit the forum for lots of answers.

My face has improved immensely over the past few months. I had complete right facial paralysis for six months. Over the summer, my smile returned and looks pretty good—if I may say so myself. This month I spent three days in Madison, Wisconsin for facial retraining with Jackie Diels (University of Wisconsin). It was amazing. I only have one thing to say about it:

NEUROMUSCULAR RETRAINING IS A MUST!!!

Well, that is one thing to say—I will add more detail in my simple, nonmedical terms. What I learned is that my facial muscles had overstrengthened as they returned. So I had a face full of Charlie horses! I learned how to stretch and release those muscles. That was painful, but has already improved and is now more relaxing. Second, I learned how to do little motions to retrain my brain and improve the synkinesis I have (inappropriate muscle movements). It was absolutely eye opening.

I am happy to be alive and just hanging out, letting my brain heal at its desired pace! I can't believe November 3 will be one year!

Since then, I have continued to visit Jackie every few months. After a couple years of hard work, the reward was Botox strategically injected to relax muscles and assist my brain with letting things go. Prior to that it was important to relax my face as much as possible to see what we had to work with regarding healing and return of movement. I considered the Botox, which relaxed tight and painful muscles, to be a reward because it allowed me to work a little less daily for a while and focus on retraining. Jackie became a friend as well as a therapist. We worked well together. In addition to the physical therapy, she was a good listener.

After a couple years of therapy, I reached an emotional low. Even though I'd heard the words that this was a lifelong process, I hadn't accepted them. Similar to my Pollyanna approach to surgery, I had to face that this was happening to me. My face would never be normal, and I had to work for what improvement I would get. I was not an exception. I went home from one session really questioning my commitment. After pouting for a few months, and feeling sorry for myself, I kicked myself and dug in again to my therapy. It is a process that requires attention constantly. I need to massage tightness from my muscles daily. I need to focus when I make certain movements. I can't smile too broadly in pictures or my smile is noticeably crooked. My face will never be normal. However, I have thanked God for the movement that did return. I thanked God for bringing Jackie into my life.

Lesson Learned

People will get sick of hearing you talk about your limitations. You will get sick of yourself if you don't adapt and focus on what you can do.

Chapter 28

It's Only
the Beginning

When I started writing about my experience, I had an idea of how it was going to turn out. It would be a neat and compact story. It would be a story of strength, miracles, and triumph. I would show the world how easily God cleaned up this little mess in my life. I would glide through surgery. I would have some pain, of course; enough to show I was STRONG. God would swoop in to execute a perfect miracle. I would be quickly healed and return to my life. I would sing His praises and show how the power of prayer had succeeded.

When God started this story, He had his own version of events that turned out to be different from my fantasy. It has been scary, and I've had my faith rocked through it. I trusted God through the whole thing, I believed in God through the whole thing, but I was puzzled by God.

I have a plaque by my fireplace that says, "Life is a journey, not a destination." I have learned that brain surgery is a journey. It is not an appendectomy. It is not a cold one gets over. Facial paralysis is filled with unexpected detours into unknown tributaries and side streams. Postsurgery head pain is filled with almost normal days followed by days or nights that are crushing with demoralizing and immobilizing pain. Single-sided deafness is more than cutting two-sided hearing in half.

Lesson Learned
Expect the unexpected.

I started writing with exuberance soon after surgery, eager to capture every detail. I assumed I was writing a story about something that would end. Something with a happy ending. Something with a painless ending. I wanted to capture my story to help people who found out they had an acoustic neuroma to know what to expect. I wanted to give people with brain tumors hope. I wanted to share an inspirational story with tumor-free people.

However, as months passed, my head continued to hurt. My face morphed from one problem to another. My hearing challenges were frustrating and at times embarrassing. I wasn't able to return to work. I had to admit disability. My energy faded. Exuberance waned as reality set in. Aimlessness and disillusion took over. Who would read such a story? It wasn't ending. I questioned the wisdom of writing a story that would, frankly, scare anyone who read it.

I wanted to share my faith and the wonderful miracle of God's love. However, as the pain continued and I folded into myself with depression and disbelief, I wondered what kind of faith I had to share. I had no miracle to show the world. The story wasn't turning out to be the story I wanted to tell. God was saying He uses little people in different ways than they choose. *Wasn't that unique?* I thought sarcastically. I was not being used at all. My life was being wasted. Telling my story would be a waste. I shelved the document. I went to Florida and walked on the beach. I pouted.

Over time, I slowed down. I started to look closer and recognized how God had cared for me. He answered unsaid prayers. Things were in place before I needed them. I wasn't the old Sally, but I had a new life that didn't always suck. I still felt pleasure. I still had my family. I listened to the nagging in my head and heart about finishing my story. Phrases would form in my head. I decided I needed a conclusion. That conclusion clearly, in my mind, involved God.

People want a testimony that shares how far down we are when God picked us up. As a teenager I was disappointed I didn't have a great testimony like the guys in the Youth for Christ movies who had overcome drugs and gangs. I had grown up in a loving Christian home. Over the next thirty years I made some bad choices despite God. I also made some really great choices I attributed to God's influence. When I did stupid things, I found I didn't want to share those bad choices publically with how God bailed me out. I grew to be a private person. My "testimony" became a philosophy lecture. Frequently, I would miss that He was right there all the time.

As I walked the beach, I pondered life. We all act like we are the first to feel love and hate, the first to experience war, the first to experience hunger and pain. However, we know the human race cycles, both as societies and individuals, through well-established patterns. The Bible and history books are filled with stories of human experiences that could be easily updated with today's names.

So what does make us special? And what makes me special? Individual experiences and choices are unique. Thus making life a big "If-Then-Else" statement. God takes pleasure in our existence. He observes and hopes we choose the right path in our individual lives; even as He already knows the choices we will make. He provides for us as we navigate this broken and fragmented world. He won't eliminate the tough stuff but will provide purpose and direction. Somehow He takes pleasure in my life, even after brain surgery.

We all get wrapped up trying to answer questions that are unanswerable. We learn to have faith in God and trust He has the best answer for us. I heard a quote, "His no is better than our yes," and formulated my own phrase, "His view is better than ours." I am angry I got a brain tumor. I am angry my head still hurts. I am angry and embarrassed my face doesn't work right. It is what it is. I can't figure it out. I do know God takes pleasure in my life. Pleasure in each little success as I climb the recovery cliff. I've learned to ask the Holy Spirit for help with my prayers.

So, I just breathe. I accept what for me are the basic facts of my faith. God is. Jesus died for me. All else is noise. This might be a repeat for mankind, but it is a unique experience for me. He takes pleasure in my life.

As the desire to continue my story grew, I began to wonder. Maybe if just knowing God's love is enough for me, maybe that would be enough to share. Maybe that would be enough for someone scared because they have just found out they have a brain tumor, or didn't have the outcome they expected. They know it will hurt. Their head is spinning with medical jargon and they just need simple. So here it is. Inhale. Exhale. Where is God? Right here.

The year 2010 marked the end of the intense portion of my story. Things have been rather static since then. I wondered how to share this story as well as how to end it. Being in an ongoing recovery mode for years is hard to capture in a riveting, continuing saga. So I chose to reflect upon what my new definition of success was. A return to the woods, where life is peaceful and I could breathe, was my new measure of accomplishment.

Chapter 29

Return to the Woods

One day in October, I decided I was ready to go alone back to the woods with my dogs. I went through my usual morning routine. Wake up. Take morning drugs. Go back to bed. Rise again and take a hot shower providing steady hot water on my head. Slowly prepare to face the day. Watch the temperature until it looked just right after lunch.

It was a sunny fall day, unseasonably warm. It had been almost a year since my surgery. I loaded my very excited dogs into the car and drove a couple miles to the nature preserve. We returned to our favorite walking place; the woods where I had prepared for surgery. The sanctuary that made me feel alive. After parking, I got two wiggly bodies into harnesses, and headed out. Alone, just the three of us. Maxalt pain pills in my pocket. Eye drops in another. Cell phone and driver's license in case of emergency. Water bottles strapped to my waist. You would think I was going for a ten-mile hike rather than a tentative and short venture into the edge of the woods.

We walked slowly at first. The dogs sniffed every tree as I took halting steps. My brain seized within my skull with each step. I inhaled and exhaled to relax my body. I lowered my shoulders and held my head as still as possible and moved in what my daughters and I called the beauty queen walk years ago as we giggled in front of the TV. Slowly, I was able to move my focus from internal pain and anxiety to things external. The woods were starting their fall coloring and were full of life. The air was fresh and woodsy.

Slowly, one step at a time, I proceeded. With each step I felt a bit stronger and my head jarred just a little less. My speed picked up. My confidence grew. Further into the woods we went. I started to outpace the sniffing dogs.

Inhale. Exhale. *I was back*. Changed forever, but back. Not free from pain but learning to adapt. Deaf on one side, with constant ringing, but hearing Nature's sounds. An ear that couldn't hear but a brain that worked hard to sort through confusion to process sounds. Birds chirped. Leaves rustled. I paused and listened to the silent beauty of the woods. Treasuring hearing but seeking silence.

One eye was dry, but able to see with a contact lens and regular eye drops. My eyes surveyed the trees clinging to summer green, but succumbing to fall's inevitable creep of color. Vines and plant leaves wound through the forest floor spreading green of different shades. The dead brown path twisted through the woods providing contrast to the vibrant greens. The sky provided glimpses of blue through high, intertwined tree branches.

I was back. Prior to surgery, I had walked these same woods in apprehension and speculation about my future. I now knew answers I hadn't predicted. I knew pain I hadn't imagined. I knew challenges that before I didn't know existed. I was different but the same. The woods change through the seasons, always different but the same.

I knew I would need a nap as payment for my outing, but that was okay. The price was fair. I would pay for the chance to walk, to breathe, to take in the woods. I knew my head would punish me for exertion, but I would pay the going price of the day.

Exhilarated at my accomplishments, I kept moving while evaluating my progress in recovery. I was on my own outing; I had redefined my independence. Inhale. Exhale. Familiar paths twisted and stretched as the terrain rose and fell. Dips challenged my balance; rises questioned my stamina.

We stopped to rest at an old wooden outlook. Familiar but new. The world was fresh to me again. I sipped water as I caught my breath. I poured water for the dogs into a little paper cup I'd tucked into my hip pack. I watched the dogs alternate between lapping water and watching the woods for activity. Paulo stood, alert, panting in the fall heat. He was a picture of contentment. Gina lay on the wooden planks, ears perked and eyes bright. Both dogs seemed to be smiling.

Lesson Learned
Life is rich.

My face couldn't smile externally, but my soul smiled broadly. *Thank you God. Thank you for my life.*

"Ready, guys? Let's go."

Epilogue

It's been over four years since my surgery. Life is good for me. I have not been able to return to work. I've adjusted to the good and bad of early retirement. My family continues to be my biggest supporters. Paulo, the little Italian Greyhound who was a big part of this story, has passed on to the big field in the sky. A summery meadow with blankets to crawl under. He is missed by me, Gina, and Gabby. Paulo's friend Chester has also gone to the meadow. Maybe they are still tangling leashes.

My head still hurts. I've learned to manage and contain my head pain through Botox, Gabapentin, Topamax, Ketoprofen, Maxalt, and lots of rest. I have explored many alternative treatments for my head pain. Some were logical, others wacky. None have helped enough for me to return to my prior life. Massage is the only thing that gives relief as it relaxes my tense muscles. Chiropractic care helps to keep my body properly aligned.

Evidently there is a small percentage of patients who have ongoing headaches following acoustic neuroma surgery. My dura, the lining of my brain, was damaged and somehow interacts negatively with the nerves of my head and neck.

My pronunciation has improved over time so my b's came *Back*. I do find that when I talk fast the lack of control is noticeable, at least to me. I can't rub my lips together to spread balm like most people, still use straws, and have a crooked smile.

Facial therapy is an ongoing part of my life now. Botox helps with my synkinesis and tightness. I remember meeting a nurse at Mayo who told me she'd suffered from Bell's palsy and her face had improved but never returned to normal. I remember lying in bed with a half-paralyzed face, thinking I saw nothing strange about her and feeling hopeful. Now I am in her place, still seeing all the flaws and "not normal" aspects of my face but being told by the people in my life, "You would never know."

I'm learning to accept the new me.

Timeline

Sep — Learned about tumor

Learned that treatment would be surgery — Oct

Nov. 3: Surgery Date — Nov — 2 Weeks: First Outing – stitches and physical therapy for face

3 Weeks: Live Alone Again; Walk to Mailbox — Dec — 1 Month: Massage, Therapy for depression; shopping in wheelchair

7 Weeks: walked around block

Jan — 2 Months: Faced Disability

2-1/2 Months: First flight to Florida — Feb — 3 Months: Mayo Checkup; Start Meds

4 Months: walk in woods w/ family — Mar

Apr — 5 Months: Car trip to Florida

May

Jun — 7 Months: First facial movement

8 Months: Meds not working — Jul

Aug — 9 Months: ANA Symposium, Mayo Clinic, new med plan

Sep

11 Months: Started Facial Therapy — Oct — 11 Months: Walked in woods ALONE

Appendix 2

Caregiver Tips

Things Kayla and I learned about being a successful caregiver:

1. Take care of yourself. If you end up sick, you won't be any help to the person who is actually recovering.
2. Be the patient's advocate. Go to doctor appointments with the AN patient. It is hard to remember what questions to ask, or even to remember the answers, when you are still trying to grasp the fact you have a brain tumor.
3. In the hospital, be an advocate for the AN patient. You will fill the gap left between nursing care and the many little needs that come up at the hospital.
4. Stay in the hospital overnight if possible to care for the patient. I found something almost always came up AFTER the nurse left.

5. In the hospital, learn where the ice chips, snacks, linens are stored. Many times you can get what the patient needs without having to call a nurse.

6. Write things down in a notebook that is always handy. Track whatever you can. Having notes on names, dates, and information will be helpful. Always keep it with you because you never know when you will need to refer back for clarification or reach out to a contact person.

7. Track pain meds both at the hospital and at home. It may seem easy to remember you took something at a particular time and can take more pain medication at a specific time, but the patient will become confused and forget. Especially when on narcotics.

8. Have a clock clearly visible to the patient. When recovering, a five-minute nap might feel like five hours. It will help the patient feel oriented.

9. If the hospital doesn't have one, bring in a white board with date and activities (for goals). It is helpful to track activities each day. It is also a good way to set goals and see which ones were met (walking, for example).

10. You may want to make meals ahead to freeze for when you get home. The first few days will be pretty hectic.

11. Have someone organize meals for you to ensure friends aren't all bringing dinner on the same night.

12. Seek out other caregivers. The ANA website has a great forum with an area specific to caregivers.

13. Help the patient do a lot of research ahead of time. It can be scary to read about what might happen, but you will be better informed when quick decisions about after care come up. I had only read about eyelid weights a few days before I

went to the hospital. When it was suggested in the hospital, I understood what they were talking about.

14. Be assertive if necessary to get enough information to understand the doctors and nurses.

15. Have a good handoff if caregivers change over the first couple weeks. That will ensure whoever is care giving has all the information needed. Details on medication schedule, eating, resting, and any limitations should be discussed.

16. Encourage the patient to continually stretch to new distances, times, or whatever they are working on. Encouragement is an amazing way to get a patient to walk around the halls one more time, sit up just a little bit longer, or to eat a little more food.

17. LISTEN A LOT.

Acknowledgments

I appreciate my Kalamazoo Christian Critique group who encouraged me to push forward with my story. Thank you, Peter DeHaan, for your encouragement to publish and assistance with details. I appreciate Amanda Rooker (and her team) for amazing feedback and very thorough editing.

Marian Thompson encouraged me as I reached out, vulnerably, with a chapter at a time to test how my story would read. To my friends of many years, Margie Stinson, Mary Koster, and Nancy Piper—what I can say? You have stood by me and continually demonstrated to me that love is laughter. Nancy Wilson has been the sister that I never had, and the rock that I've needed and turned to many times.

I want to thank the doctors and nurses at Mayo Clinic in Rochester, Minnesota, for their incredible skill, compassion, and care. I am still in awe of the care that I received from each person that I came in contact with. Thank you for doing the jobs that you do.

Thank you to the Acoustic Neuroma Association for providing incredible information during my search for data. The forum provided camaraderie, support, and many answers.

Thank you to all the friends and colleagues who followed my blog and sent encouragement in kind, funny, or thoughtful words. Words cannot describe the warmth that fueled my recovery through your continued checking in. Lastly, but closest to my heart, I want to thank my family for their incredible support throughout this process.

About the Author

Sally Stap is a writer living in Michigan. She began her writing career after brain surgery brought her information technology career to a halt. The tumor quickly sidelined her life after surgery and a long, ongoing recovery. Struggling with head pain, facial paralysis, and single-sided deafness, she turned to writing to capture her experience. Her right brain, which had been demanding to be heard, is now regularly exercised through writing.

Sally is a member of the Kalamazoo Christian Writer's critique group as well as the Wordweavers and FaithWriters organizations. Sally published magazine articles on outsourcing and pharmaceutical regulatory issues during her years as an IT consultant. She also spent a considerable part of her career interpreting information technology jargon for business organizations through written documentation and oral presentations. She now strives to interpret emotions and experiences into words. She maintained a blog throughout her diagnosis, surgery, and recovery period in order to interact with the people in her life.

She creates word combinations in her head while walking her Italian greyhound, Gina, in a nearby land preserve. She formulates ways to share emotions while playing with her grandson. She brainstorms story ideas while hanging out with her youngest daughter, Kendra. She logically explores ways to capture experiences with Kayla, her older daughter. She patiently opens and closes the back door for her meowing half-Siamese cat, Gabby.

She learned to laugh at herself after learning that a sense of humor helps to nurture a better temperament than frustration. "Accept that the future you is still undefined. Recovery takes time."

Printed in the USA
CPSIA information can be obtained
at www.ICGtesting.com
LVHW090220020424
776145LV00005B/201